SIGNAL FROM DRACO

Mebane Robertson spent his formative years in Richmond, Virginia, and New Orleans, Louisiana. A graduate of The College of William & Mary and Long Island University, he resides in New York where he is a Ph.D. student in English literature at Fordham University. His poems have been widely published in both print and online publications, including *The Beloit Poetry Journal, Blue Unicorn, Guernica, The Journal, The Lyric, Mudfish, Poetalk,* and many more. He has recorded eleven CDs to date and plays many venues in New York City. After a chapbook collection, Black Widow Press is pleased to present Mr. Robertson's first book of collected poems highlighting both recent writings and poems written and published over the last fifteen years.

Dr. Gale Swiontkowski is Professor of English at Fordham University. Her specialty is modern poetry. Besides numerous articles, her recent publications include *A New Species of Man: The Poetic Persona of W. B. Yeats,* which won the Bucknell University Press Prize in Contemporary Literary Criticism, and *Imagining Incest: Sexton, Plath, Rich, and Olds on Life with Daddy.* Dr. Swiontkowski is working on a book tentatively titled *Antaeus: Poetry and the Analogical Imagination.*

SIGNAL FROM DRACO

New and Selected Poems

Mebane Robertson

with an Introduction by
Gale Swiontkowski

Black Widow Press
Boston, MA

BLACK WIDOW PRESS is an imprint of Commonwealth Books, Inc., Boston. All Black Widow Press books are printed on acid-free paper, glued and sewn into bindings.
JOSEPH S. PHILLIPS, Publisher
www.blackwidowpress.com

Cover Photo: *Cat's Eye Nebula* ©NASA, ESA, HEIC, and The Hubble Heritage Team (STScI/AURA)
Book Design by Kerrie Kemperman

ISBN-13: 978-0-9795137-0-1
ISBN-10: 0-9795137-0-7

Library of Congress Cataloging-in-Publication Data

Robertson, Mebane, 1967–
    Signal from draco : new and selected poems / Mebane Robertson. — Black Widow Press ed.
    p. cm.
    ISBN-13: 978-0-9795137-0-1
    I. Title

Printed by Thomson-Shore
Printed in the United States

10 9 8 7 6 5 4 3 2 1

For Linda, Layne, and Julie

ACKNOWLEDGEMENTS

The following poems first appeared in these journals:

The Ampersand: "The Bucket and the Butterfly," "Hello," and "Burns' Woes"

Beloit Poetry Journal: "Subject Body 1-4"

Blue Unicorn: "Subject Body 18"

Downtown Brooklyn: "Of Cups and Balls, Coins and Cards," "The Catenary," "The Whole Way Home," "Tonight is June," and "The Pariah"

Guernica: "Doctor of Teeth (White, Natasha)"

The Journal: "Ambiguous Numbers" and "Dark Channels"

The Lyric: "Vocation" and "Wallflower"

MPWA 1998 Daybook: "The War Between Green and Orange" and "Swallowtail, Your Slightest Touch"

Mudfish: "Passage," "It Has Been So Long Now," and "Imago Stage"

Poetalk: "Just Off the Coast," "Silver Toe Ring," "Devil's Tower," and "Full-Length Mirror"

CONTENTS

Introduction

Seating Chart • 1

The War Between Green and Orange • 2

Another Goodbye • 3

The Whole Way Home • 4

Between Beds • 5

Flyer to Flyer • 6

Photo • 7

Visitors' Room • 8

Keeping the Cage • 9

Nearly Drawn from Life • 10

Please Don't Be Long • 11

Doctor of Teeth (White, Natasha) • 12

Tonight the Law • 13

St. Croix Sun Stroke • 14

The Bucket and the Butterfly • 15

Imago Stage • 16

South Boston Border • 19

Gaseous Vertebrate • 20

Someone Left the Program Running • 22

Down the Music • 23

Way of the Dolphins • 24

4/7 Psalm • 25

Just Off the Coast • 26

Of Being In The Truth • 27

Black Ringlets • 28

03/27 Poem (Fordham Library) • 29

Stage of Sorts • 30

Double Egypt Surprise • 31

Longer Than Your Sleeve • 32

3/28 Poem • 33

Variables • 34

Another Stone • 35

Dumb ● 36

The Hymn Ward ● 37

The Ruins ● 38

Strata ● 40

Yard Man ● 41

The Clover Patch ● 42

Two up from Dog Star ● 44

The Corner ● 45

Bouncing Off Clouds (Technique 14-B) ● 46

For "Emily Glass," Wherever I May... ● 47

Scribe ● 48

Second Guessing ● 49

Small Craft Advisory ● 50

During Yoga Class ● 51

The Resistance ● 52

The Conflict ● 53

Summer Cottage ● 54

Hello ● 55

Subject Body ● 57

The Hierarchy ● 77

Dreams of Cursive Ringlets ● 78

28 Willow Street ● 79

Dark Channels ● 80

Friday Night ● 81

Days Before the War ● 82

Outside ● 83

Silver Toe Ring ● 84

The One Stroke ● 85

Burning the Trash ● 86

Travelers ● 87

Burns' Woes ● 88

Dreaming Along the Promenade (11th Floor) ● 89

Trails (July 4, 2003) ● 90

It Has Been So Long Now ● 91

Plan for the Day ● 92

A Paris Sending-Off ● 93

You Who Never Were ● 94

Destination ● 95

Full Fathom ● 96

Sunday at the Pavilion ● 97

Letting it Happen ● 98

These Lives ● 99

Charted Ground ● 100

Jerusalem ● 101

Ambiguous Numbers ● 102

Fire Insurance (All Spruced Up) ● 103

Music Therapy ● 104

My Lock ● 105

The Faun's Ears ● 106

Poetic Investigations ● 107

Where We Left Off ● 108

Sebastian ● 109

Borders ● 110

Nobody Too ● 111

Today ● 112

Watertown Arsenal ● 113

Song of the Ink, Feathers, and Fowl ● 114

The Machine ● 115

An Oath ● 116

The Donkey's Dream ● 119

The Large Glass ● 120

Book of Laws ● 121

Part of the Hitch ● 122

Turn the Key and See ● 123

Guitar ● 124

O City ● 125

Revelation ● 126

"Where is Your Moses Now?" ● 127

Even as I Speak ● 128

Where the Ducks Go ● 129

Last Meetings ● 130

The Sting ● 131

The Song Ward ● 132

Exchange ● 133

Song Eleven ● 134

For a Brother ● 135

Vocation • 136

Cut Off • 137

Jane Making Rain • 138

Of Course You Can • 139

Summer is Going • 140

Vantage • 141

City Blocks You • 142

Building Outwards • 143

Due Time • 144

Pop • 145

The Door • 146

Conscience • 147

Moving • 148

Wintertime Love • 149

Wallflower • 150

The Roundabout • 153

Audit for the Fire Delayed • 154

The Meeting • 155

The Roof of Bellevue • 156

Not so Funny • 157

Stumble of an Operative • 158

That Group's Feet • 159

In The Halls • 160

Interlude in Shower Tile Green • 161

Somewhere, Somehow • 162

Swallowtail, Your Slightest Touch • 163

The Good Mechanic • 164

The Pariah • 165

Another Extreme • 166

Tonight is June • 167

Some Other Lives • 168

So Winter Ends • 169

Quiet One • 170

So Vast, So Beautiful A Land • 171

Should I Call Her This Soon • 172

Full-Length Mirror • 173

River's Flowing ● 174

Random Bees ● 175

Restraint and Seclusion ● 176

Pre-Recorded Messages ● 179

Prove It Then ● 180

Moving to Mauve Room (Device 32) ● 181

Professional School ● 182

Boy ● 184

Passage ● 185

One Martini ● 186

Firm Convictions ● 187

Notes Toward a Better Life ● 188

Trophies of the Sun ● 189

The Maze Behind the Palace ● 190

Monster de la Now ● 191

Milk of Eyes ● 192

Milady's (10:00 P.M.) ● 193

Mauve Mud Pie ● 194

Love Keeps Going ● 195

Karlheinz on the Cover ● 196

I Turn Away ● 197

The Flight ● 198

Growing Thin as Process ● 199

Green Wilding ● 200

Fancy Clothes and These are Roses ● 201

Resignation ● 202

Dialogue Involving Garments and Accessories ● 203

Devil's Tower ● 204

Delusions From A Bus Window ● 205

Testimony for Someone Silver ● 206

The Catenary ● 207

Of Cups and Balls, Coins and Cards ● 208

Come Down In Time ● 209

Hassling Kooks ● 210

Between the Clock and the Bed ● 211

As a Mirror is Believed ● 212

PUBLISHER'S PREFACE

I am pleased to present the first title in the Black Widow Press New Poets Series, *Signal from Draco: New and Selected Poems* by Mebane Robertson. I first met Mr. Robertson more than ten years ago in the French Quarter of New Orleans, and still have and admire his first chapbook of poems, *Watertown Arsenal,* from that time period. Over the years, his poems have been published in numerous forums both under his own name and various "aliases," as he cared less to whom the poems were attributed than that the poems went into circulation and were read. Also a songwriter and musician, Mebane has obtained an underground, but growing audience (despite his unconventional and somewhat raspy voice) because of his powerful and intriguing lyrics, honed by his poet's ear. First and foremost, though, he remains a dedicated poet and writer. This collection, culled from more than 2,000 of Mebane's poems written over the last fifteen years, depicts a wide range of styles and a remarkably singular voice. It is a voice that stands out amongst the piles of manuscripts one sees as a publisher. I thank you for picking up this volume and hope you enjoy Mebane's poems and this new series.

Joseph S. Phillips
Publisher
Black Widow Press
Boston, MA

INTRODUCTION

Once, in a poetry workshop I attended during the first Gulf War, the poet/teacher told us students that political poems were not possible anymore. In a later workshop, we heard from another poet that the word "feeling" cannot be used in poems anymore, because Mr. Rogers (Frederick McFeely Rogers, that is) had ruined it. True, poets must always cope with the uses to which other, less linguistically sensitive people put their material. Poetry is always seeking to "make it new,"[1] often to rescue language from its own rapture. But in doing so, many contemporary poets have become somewhat cynical about the possibilities of language and rather jaded about the themes poetry might still address. As Franz Wright recently put it, "...our culture is riddled with irony. It's sick with it... There's an absence of any tragic sense."[2]

T. S. Eliot, lamenting the "immense panorama of futility and anarchy which is contemporary history," famously pronounced:

> ...it appears likely that poets in our civilization, as it exists at present, must be difficult. Our civilization comprehends great variety and complexity, and this variety and complexity, playing upon a refined sensibility, must produce various and complex results. The poet must become more and more comprehensive, more allusive, more indirect, in order to force, to dislocate, if necessary, language into his meaning.[3]

Thus, we have poets like John Ashbery, who seems in the prevailing opacity of his poems to follow Eliot's direction, but also poets like Seamus Heaney, who has said the poet "should stick to the energies of generation in [his] own language."[4] Surely, both applications of language are necessary: poets must transport language into new territories (Draco, perhaps?) yet acknowledge this language as the medium of us all.

---

[1] Ezra Pound uses this phrase in various texts, including *The Cantos* and the volume of essays *Make It New.*
[2] From an interview in *Image* 51 (Fall 2006): 76.
[3] From *Selected Prose of T.S. Eliot* (NY: Farrar, Straus and Giroux, 1975), p. 177, 65.
[4] From the audiotape *Seamus Heaney and Tom Paulin* (London: Faber & Faber, 1983). Heaney uses this phrase when commenting on his errant choice of the standard English phrase "flax dam" over the more regionally familiar "lint hole" in the poem "Death of a Naturalist."

This double awareness is the strength, I believe, of Mebane Robertson's *Signal from Draco*. Many of the poems in this volume are "difficult," but together they create their own environment, or (as William Carlos Williams would have it) their own "weather."[5] Each poem feeds into a ground that gives rise to another poem, and if one poem in isolation might be puzzling, the poems together speak a language that we learn and know and come to understand, intuitively if not rationally. This volume sports a very interactive, organic internal structure. Words and images from different poems communicate, and through these connections, these facets, our understanding expands. (I recommend that you note in particular the recurring imagery of feathers and birds throughout this volume.) Yet the external structure is equally intriguing: the sectioning of the poems into five parts, each with its own characteristics, each bumping up against and talking back to the others. Yes, a poem stands on its own, in this volume, as in the work of any poet. But a poem speaks perhaps even more persuasively within a larger context, as one pixel in the complex panorama of a fine poet.

At times, poems are considered good only if they are nearly incomprehensible—if we can't understand them, they must be works of genius; or if we can understand them, we must be geniuses. Many of Mebane Robertson's poems obliquely address the issue of complexity versus comprehensibility and our contradictory expectations of modern poems, in part by participating ironically in the modern obliquity. Images of fragmentation frequent the poems ("Now remained two wrists, like broken / Rained on sculpture, fixed, two stalks of fingers," pg 7), suggesting the dissociated state of the modern splintered personality, our J. Alfred Prufrock. In some respects, this is simply an honest depiction of the complexity of modern consciousness, in a world lacking a communally accepted unifying spiritual agent. Post-Darwin, post-Nietzsche, we seem to be "Always monkeying / In God's rafters" (pg 32). In a poem titled "Nearly Drawn from Life," we get a post-Freudian glimpse of the unintegrated self on a New York City subway car: "Numb, drowning in the rumble, silent signals / Faltering in a shared matrix / Of visitors hearing a nervous God playing / Earth's set of kettledrums under the Devil's baton" (pg 10). Here's another purgatorial vision of the modern self:

---

[5] See the essay "Against the Weather," in *Selected Essays* (NY: New Directions, 1969), p. 196-219.

When the duplicate of my love
Confuses herself over the machine...
After several hours sorting through
Various proofs to find which one
She is, she leaves it to me to judge—
To me who has already been
Through the machine and no
Longer can distinguish myself
From my many imposters. (pg 115)

If we are all Jobs in a world of divine irresponsibility or invisibili-ty, in a world in which "Psyche's doppel is downed and grounded" and "Yin and Yang have two eyes for Picasso's pleasure" (15), we do well to turn to art for some sense of order and meaning. Yes, art may ape the disorder, as some of these poems do, but in its very existence on a page or a canvas, an art form embodies place, stance, statement, order. Through art, the best of us can accept and play with our inherent dis-order, jazzing a reality that is complex and ironic and often deeply pleasurable to our modern sensibilities. Mebane has told me that the artist who has most influenced his work as painter, musician, and poet is Picasso. Fragmentation in the hands of an accomplished artist becomes powerful emotion: grief sometimes, celebration other times. As Mebane would have it, "My hand can't yet seem to wave / Good-bye to the Righteous, nor can it quit shaking / This Devil's pair of carved bone dice" (pg 25). Moreover,

I could go on forever about this soulless soul
Who has guided me into one majorly weedy, snaky harbor—
The one who has left me at the wheel to shake us loose.
To think, in another life, I could have been a greeting card
Sweet and banal, mass-produced in all my pastel glory,
And here I am, my maker asleep. In this darkness I press on (52)

Just who is this "I" who seems to inherit the undoable job of God? Ay, that's the question. And the answer is, all of us, of course—each individual sailing (or not) through her life. We are often tempted to quit this impossible task, to feel sorry for ourselves:

> I seem guided by some agency, quite singular,
> Which uses me to escape from his or her sundry fears.
> I have grown tired of being used as such. Where's
> The payback? If you see who or whatever made me,
> Tell it, or him, or her I will no longer play the pawn. (53)

What can we do when we are allowed "Minimal Post King James Verbal Activity" (46)? We can protest, get irreverent, give up in spite:

> Longing helps you figure what you need, for real.
> But so does suffering get-what-you-pay-for wisdom.
> The book tells us this. Blah. Blah to the books.
> Your wrist keeps your hand attached
>
> To the rest of your nice body, not
> For easy exits and departures, before the scene
> Ends with a player balled in a cold pool of blood.
> Ball up this page. Toss it into the darkening wings. (30)

But in the end we are happier not to be "Locked into this one and only face, / Locked into this one and only voice" (pg 9), to be instead the multifaceted, cubistic Dora, the jumble that faces several directions and somehow coheres. In a sense, we make our own redemption by remaking ourselves in art:

> Are your hands strong enough to wash away
> These troubles you've carried around today,
> In one form or another,
> Though each different from the other?
> ...Was there ever a scarecrow that was healed? (35)

The long sequence of poems titled "Subject Body," which constitutes part two of this volume, is its centerpiece—a sustained exploration of the issue of identity, in the form of poetic autobiography. Think of the implications of the title alone. First, there's the mix of abstract idea and concrete thing—to what extent am "I" the idea of myself I carry in my head, to what extent my body? Then there's the play on the first word: the body as the subject of the poet and poem, body as subject to poet and poem and other people and powers. The poems that follow this provocative title constitute a self-conscious self-analysis—not Mebane Robertson's analysis of himself as an historical being, but the kind of activity we all should be performing to remain responsible individuals within society, responsible to the other (hopefully) responsible individuals within society. "Subject Body" is also thus an imagistic autobiography, as poem glints off poem (each one, one uniform block of eleven lines) to give us a faceted presentation of self, again reminiscent of Picasso's cubist paintings. ("...'Picasso started / At the center and worked out, / So our abstract space is parted / With what we humans are about,'" pg 143.) There are archaic sentence structures and increasingly frequent capitalizations as the sequence unfolds, reminiscent perhaps of the identity agonies in a sentimental novel. But the speaker addresses himself not only in third person initially but, even more removed, as "Subject Body," as compound concept/thing to be analyzed from a distance.

Yet within this formal artifice of structure and tone, identity itself is probed and played with and taunted and not tamed. "Off to Church went the Subject each Sunday morn— // ...Subject jestered / His Calling" (#12, pg 60). Although the subject is at first presented in third person, it grows more familiar as the poems progress: "Subject," "Subject B.," "Sub- Sub- Stubject Body." The speaker, as his subject ages, is able to play more, jest more, improvise more with the subject's identity. Later in the sequence, we confront the first person, but in sly form: "I / (Subject's ventriloquism)" (#42, pg 70). There are references also to the first person plural and provocative phrases like "Subject, speaking from the First Persons... / I think he liked them" (#41, pg 70) and "I unto You" (#39, pg 69), which raise all sorts of appropriate confusions about the boundaries of an individual identity. At the end of # 50, toward the end of the sequence, we read, "This One I Meant More than the Others. No Lie" (73). This what?—this self, this poem, this half-truth? Truth cannot be pinned down to one truth; self cannot be pinned down to one self, one identity. "Young Body served, he told himself, a faction injured / Who saw God in the eyes of scattered birds— / Out of bounds already, ever opening wider" (#6, pg 58). (Birds again!) "Subject Body's throat was broken open / To let loose a Blackbird with yellow eyes" (#44, pg 71). (Wasn't it a pie, once upon a time?) Or, if you're happier with scales than feathers:

Subject Body swallowed the Lovely Bait.
He Played Out Hard only to be Landed in the Keel.
He was Admired for the Sheen of his Silver Scales,
And Weighed for Confirmation before being Thrown
Back in the Dark Waters that had Spawned Him.
He was a Pawn of the Worms and the Weather,
Lily Pads were his Haunt, Through which the Boat
Shadowed the Surface, Stirred the Long Stems.
Fishers of Men Netted Folk of the Rainy Bank,
And Red Letter Edition Ink dripped and Pooled.
Subject Body Spat Out the Inky Words. (#46, pg 72)

That, right there, may be the ideal autobiography—one that has been lived before, by other subject bodies. Certainly one of the paradoxes of identity is the answers we find when we become subject to other powers, when we voluntarily play the inspired pawn. Hamlet finally learned that.

I've spoken of poems mainly from parts one and two of *Signal from Draco*. Let me finish by commenting briefly on how the poems from these initial parts set up the poems that follow. The informality and irregularity in form and tone and theme of part one are echoed in part three; the regularity in form and tone and theme of part two are echoed in part four. Part five marries the two. In all, we see the complexity of truth and the truth in complexity. Just as a word is a shaped grunt or scream, this volume merges form and confusion, comprehensibility and incomprehensibility: "I am are two words to begin the begin" (pg 84)—no longer the Word in the Beginning, though we participate in that process. I particularly recommend the quasi-prophetic poems of part four, especially "The Donkey's Dream" (pg 119) and "Vocation" (pg 136), poems in which something like rhymed nonsense speaks wisdom, much like Shakespeare's fools.

But because this identity work is a never-ending process, let's leave it at this: "And what's really there will always be there, / Though outside of the picture, outside / Of even the frame" (pg 168).

—Gale Swiontkowski
Professor and Associate Chair, English
Fordham University

SEATING CHART

The windows here, the three of them,
Open in evening to a sycamore top
That repeatedly drops its carved leaves
Onto the sidewalk passersby use, lick (the leaves)
In gusts around the brainpans of hapless neighbors.
A spider's thread connects,
Trembling like arthritic fingers
Of an old man at a folding table.
A stray eyelash blows down and drifts
Onto the pale heart inside the stranger's open palm.
Some guests are givens; some, some they surprise.

THE WAR BETWEEN GREEN AND ORANGE

Tagged 'em in a web, he shows
The littlest soldiers through the tiny door.

Draped rich with praise, they caress
Their small stars, eat the rooty bank like suitors.

The way the wind blew that night,
I doubted I should ever make it home.

What now little man? Unstring the nerve network?
Laser the orbit's doll-eyed iris?

I planted this thing, knowing it would grow—
Fennel and indigo, a pumpkin in the path.

Small spots the privates keep scrubbing,
Traces in the hot-house, Isotope dye.

ANOTHER GOODBYE

Here is a chance to finally say
I'm not the fool people think.
No. They didn't say it to my face.
That's not entirely true, the to my face
Part, but I get the gist in their tone.
No. I wasn't a mirror reflecting back—
And so claiming my own private wisdom.
Nor do I claim people are jealous of me.
I don't understand people
In their long, dark scarves
People wink their blue eyes—
Bluer than the gray river below—
As if they were aware
Of my great and final destination.

THE WHOLE WAY HOME

You leaned hard into luck. Luck leaned away.
Yesterday was, after all, a two-headed cow—an attachment
You were forbidden to open. Too many cracked mirrors,
Bridges bombed, too many pumpkins in the field.

What's healed only healed with time.
Like the doctor's legend of the perfectly sweet, perfectly clear onion
That, once unearthed, proved to be
Neither perfectly sweet nor perfectly clear.

And where does that stuff end and the better part begin?
And what of heat lightning over the hills.
And what of telephones shaped like bananas? Stupid questions
To which the past answers, "Come in. Come in."

Even now I can glimpse through the black eye slits
Those eyes the color of no color, those eyes the color the fog
That settles now as I fill out this application
Accounting for certain strange and mostly missing years.

BETWEEN BEDS

Sometime quiet moments sneak up on us
Usually when the day is ending,
And one goes over the evening's hours
Like snow shaken in a child's winter toy.
And the past waves goodbye like a lover
In long white gloves we'll never touch again.
And the ship carries us off into days
Where dragons and monsters bargain over
What remains to be written of our lives,
And while the vessel sails on steadily,
The compasses of our hearts are spinning
Like the carousels of wild youth
Faster and faster until we can hold
On no longer and fly off each in turn, over
The most distant of horizons, now and forever.

FLYER TO FLYER

Recognize your marks—water towers
Strung along the blonde cape, splinters

In your back, and acetylene
Crowning the gap like Gabriel's flame.

You love the loveless peaks and troughs;
Seeding burnt clouds. You love less

These thin wires of candy. You stonewall
The stencil the House of David provided.

Powder blue she came to me,
Dubbing me Central, powder blue she came.

I know you've got half a mind
To shoulder that thing. You smoke too much

In your bubble, just one of the gang.
Ball's in your court. Maintain radio silence.

PHOTO

They held the remains of each other's hands
Where she cropped the picture just so,
Where their hands were woven together.
Now remained two wrists, like broken
Rained on sculpture, fixed, two stalks of fingers.
It doesn't catch the flame of her cheek and eye.
Both eyes she burned out to a pure black hollow.
Blood cannot easily re-enter the body once it's spilt.
It would be like trying to purify the oceans
By starting with the oceans themselves,
Instead of the running, red rivers that fatten them.
Most of this is lost in the shadows.
I am sorry, my last friend. It is best this way.

VISITORS' ROOM

For his sake, she is falling
  Down,
            And down
          Through a muffled black shaft
Where one with a severe
        Estimate of how much she can take,
            Laughs an ugly laugh.
In the thin
            Sharpening of knives,
The knives of memory's kitchen,
The stroking
    Of steel on stone,

        She leans back over the glass-
        Topped wall
To glimpse all the men she loved once
Who step, one after another, into
    A long black bus
Instead of her, or more exactly,
            In her place
To be taken quietly, without force,

        Away forever.

KEEPING THE CAGE

Why like big cats do we growl and tear—
Claws slicing the air—at one another,
Each unto each, while the black nets of hunger
And gluttony are thrown by hands beyond
Our comprehension—the ringleaders
Leaving our attitudes to be our only freedom,
Locked into this one and only face,
Locked into this one and only voice,
A total eclipse of all we call the sun
That won't let us see the sky and clouds
Assuming the forms of beguiling animals
With long, triplicate, standard gray tails?

NEARLY DRAWN FROM LIFE

Bound, seated, rooted in a new row of citizens
Who, like wild mushrooms in a forest,
Flare and sink into themselves like corn stalks
In husks of yellow or other colored hair
Blaring the muted trumpets of each the other's words
Never to be spoken out loud,
Who are caught in the clatter of the NYC #4 train,
Numb, drowning in the rumble, silent signals
Faltering in a shared matrix
Of visitors hearing a nervous God playing
Earth's set of kettledrums under the Devil's baton.

PLEASE DON'T BE LONG

You are shifting on a bench out of range
Of the University Writing Center where
No one but the teacher is required
To say more than a few, terse words to you.

You perceive; you do not judge. In turn,
You are cuffed by a large, blind machine
Called Humanity, which at one time
Was something of which you were still a part.

DOCTOR OF TEETH (WHITE, NATASHA)

I had this steel drafting pencil behind my ear
Which must have slipped out while
I dozed and performed random violence for evidence
On a scratch pad during a fugue.

Some jackass gets lashed behind the curtain
And guess who catches the flak.
It's lonely it's getting harder
To do the dirty work of ever getting them back.

Gardener brushed the willow with tar,
Which on a phase-shifted wavelength we "did it" under
Slowly on some pills
The Angel of Minor Tranqs had cheeked that week.

In the service it's good for my hands
Not to know what each other are doing, but the agency
Wants to update my file and run some Rhine tests. I told them,
Before you lock the door, make sure I'm actually inside this time.

TONIGHT THE LAW

Tonight the law shakes loose its black teeth,
Around which eddy rock gray froth.
The expert is consulting dental records—
The black marks of chapters and verses.

Tonight the black letters dance
Deep in a wood, uncrossed t's and undotted i's,
Deep through a bramble while the law gnashes
Past thorny brakes, the omega awakens.

Tonight the omega awakens; tonight it is told
The law is after it, like unto a pack of hounds.
Consulting the black letters of the chapter,
The expert is deep in rock gray froth.

Deep through the brambles, the teeth shake loose,
Shake as each falls into place.
Omega says we need more time, deep in the wood.
The black teeth wink in the rock gray froth.

ST. CROIX SUN STROKE

If you once studied habits
Enveloped in the Prince's Danish wind, there
You would find all the feathers
Of the third-crowing cocks you chased
And denied on islands you simply loved.

In a just hand, bubonically meted out,
Many want the sick to all just go away.
In the salt bay you watch the old house
Of a carpetbagger out of a proper context
Burn blue-orange plumes against the night sky.

The moon drops silver to put it all out
Like lead sifted into cooling waters
To form birdshot to finally bring down to earth
The fugitive frigate your illness brings,
Stealing fish from you, hiding too much in the open.

THE BUCKET AND THE BUTTERFLY

These notions have cropped up out of nowhere,
Without time or space, suckled in silence.
I have kept quiet far too long a time about it all:
My space, a vacuum tube of children's scissors

Cuts clear the swallowtail's wing; the patterned
Blotched, blue, smeared dots, O winged one,
Psyche's doppel is downed and grounded.
Mother Earth is at the center, strange as it sounds,

Crazed with green rivers, shining, hard to pin
Down like an unetherized specimen.
Yin and Yang have two eyes for Picasso's pleasure.
Stars don't just die, more always born anew.

Like a boy swinging a bucket filled with sand
Overhead, centrifugal force keeps the matter in.
Of course, the butterfly and the bucket collide.
This is all I know, and all that I was told to tell.

IMAGO STAGE

We move from the zinc bar to a booth—
Should we speak in the tongue
                    Of half-an-hour ago?
                              When we'd patched things up
        And present and past mixed.
You with five cosmopolitans and my three Bombay martinis,
And were laughing again, you almost hysterically.
                              Then you looked at me, in retrospect kind of funny
And asked, "Where have all the lions gone?"
                              And you looked fine in your patterned green dress.
        I haven't see you in a dress since I don't know when,
                    It became you, though I didn't say so.
And she, you said, dresses like
                    The candy suckers
        They hand out to kids at your pharmacy on Lexington.
Forget the woman at work, I've heard enough about her.
                    Let's get back to what you were telling me,
About not being yourself, and the no insurance for a decent shrink.
I know. I know. I won't use that word again.
            Then smoothly guiding us out of that cul-de-sac
                                        You say
You want a gray jag. Not any gray jag either.
                    One of the old E-Types. And, God,
I'm totally with you. The lines on those things.
                    You said that was a car for a real lion
For a real James Bond   I'm always looking for the real James Bond,
            Are you a real James Bond? You said, and it was a come on
I wanted to roll with, but it was still too soon, and too late.
            So I also start going off on lions.
Then we move onto sheep and goats
            (whose skeletons, you learned in college, can't
    Be distinguished from each other), and the metaphysics of pigs and wolves.
You've accused me of being
A wolf in sheep's clothing since high school.

16

                    Though, of course, I have no inkling what you
                    Mean.
You start going off
On Deleuze and "intensities" of "wolfness"
                    And how you can't stop reading
A Thousand Plateaus and keep a bathroom copy on the toilet top
                    And a subway copy in your bag.
After four breakdowns, that's not the word, more like expansive pirouettes
coupled off
        With nuclear core meltdowns,
                    All I can say is You're too smart for your own good.
You ask me if I've ever seen a mayfly.
                Mayfly? I think. Who the hell cares about mayflies? Like with
Most of your questions, I just say I don't know.
We order more rounds and the gallows humor
                    Gets so loud and the other tables
Were looking at us,
                    And at the way you were eating your salad,
        At times using your fingers as if you didn't
                    Care that it's simply something people don't do—
Taking a piece of feta, tossing it up, and catching it in your mouth
                    Telling me to hold up my finger so you could throw
        A sweet onion ring on it.
You stopped like you had something funny to say, getting a hold
        Of yourself, you said "Did you know
        Mayflies in their winged state of mutation, really do only live
        A day?"
                    One lousy day. Bummer. It's called imago stage.
            Living in imago stage—one day and blotto, that's that.
            You tying cherry stems into little red hearts with your tongue.
                I reminded myself I was involved with somebody.
                The world's a trap, wish I could be more like you.
                Stupid words, "I'm involved with someone."
                I know how you are in the sack.   ➤

                              17

"In the sack," God, everyone talks like everyone else,
Proximity makes people different.
I'm drunk, horny, thinking too much. Words. Hell with 'em.
I wanted you, but anyway,
Your plastered crazy self fell out of the booth. I can't say, convey, how
Funny you are on a manic high—but there was something scary about it.
I was never one to tone you down.
Everything you said was funny is all.
You asked if I wanted to come home with you.
I said Not tonight.
You went home and took (by the account I got from your sister, Linda)
A month's worth of lithium and valproic acid,
Apparently walked out on the balcony
Of your 19th floor luxury Park and 79th condo
Climbed over railing
And jumped
Out of a world,
Where there was
No lion
No James Bond
There to catch you.

SOUTH BOSTON BORDER

Off the main drag, you felt something give.
Filters blown, irrelevance creeping in—
The plaid pattern of a flowing tie,
Allergies became something weird on the wind.

Choices had to be made, between the one key
And the other. You dropped it a diminished fifth
And paralyzed a lovely choir, who had become
Your natural mother, your quench of sweet sweet tea.

Displaced and transposed, your hungry ditties
Tore up the blackest of back roads—
Tossing empties, more or less, along the shoulder.
More or less, I still wear your badge.

Now some people want to schedule some things in.
Now some people want to block in some time.
Never has such sweet age seemed half so far away.
This inward turning. These stops are scripted.

GASEOUS VERTEBRATE

Bartender cracks someone
                    Another cold one. Me?
    I'm a Scotch man.   Dried out for a good stretch—back on it now.
Wonder if it will ever be my last
              Again.   But I like the succor of Happy Hour.
Something burns like an Olympian torch,
              Held high, leading me on to whatever bar
    Will still have me.   I stare at a row of bottles
Like a Southern Belle looking in the mirror before a blind date.
              That's what it's like each time, a blind date—
Never know where the hell I'll end up,
                    Whose apartment, what gutter.   This Southern
              Belle has woken up in three different states now, always no
              Clue until someone fills me in.
                    They used to call me Scholarship Boy. Heh.
In my enforced solitude I perform random
              Operations and permutations with such things as
The names of the bottles on a certain row, give a numeric value to each letter—
              Figure out the universe, Einstein's "Constant" Crap. Heh.
              Once that wasn't just something funny.
              Once I was a different man
              Treated in a different fashion.
    Scholarships, Fellowships, Potato chips. Like to get me a bag,
But then I might not afford
                    The buy-back freebee.
                    Facts and people. I'm better with facts.
People in the next chair always seem to empty out.
                    People talk about sports. Not me. "I permit to speak at
Every hazard nature without check, with original energy." See, if
              You talk nonsense or don't know the Yankee's roster
People clear out around you.
                    The only words I'm basically allowed to utter are to signify
I need another Scotch.
              Usually I just wait till she comes round and nod.

This world's not for me. This world's a ballbuster. Not
For the tender-minded. And there's God, and the Social Democratic Agenda,
                      And Ultra-Covert Operations, and
    The woman who just came in the door yells
                          She got a fucking flat on the fucking BQE.
            And no one, of course, seems to mind her language.
If I had one wish, not to suffer the penalty (that's the thing about wishes;
always got to
            Consider the penalty even in dream wishes),
If I had that wish…. Hell, I think I'll go on and get me that bag of chips.

SOMEONE LEFT THE PROGRAM RUNNING

—I mean
                I'm all talked out on business for the night. This limo
     Smells like a hearse. Did I tell you about your age
I worked in a funeral parlor, as they were called.
                —Sir, do you mind if I crack open the mini-bar?
—Go ahead, boy. You were hell on wheels
                         In there with those figures.
     How the hell you pull those
                              Numbers outa your ass?
     You got some kind of microchip up there? I'm just razzing you, boy.
     But that was some curve ball
                         You threw them.   Shoulda seen the look
     On that guy's face. Pay good money for a picture of it.
                Now
I'm thinking if we downsize that one segment.
                         What group was that?
     You've got the papers, check…
—Scotch and soda, Sir?
                —Yeah. Yeah. Whatever. I mean. And that snide little
Smartass punk working the lame assed presentation.
                         I'd like to give him
          A swift kick in his techno ass. Smartass punk.
     Putting on airs.
                              Like we were in kindergarten.
Like it was Romper Room or something.
                         O what the hell. Did you notice…?
     —Your Scotch and soda, Sir.
—Did you say soda? The hell with soda.
                Give me three fingers, neat.
                —We do have that meeting with Henley at nine a.m., Sir.
—To hell with Henley. And quit that "Sir" shit,
          You've been Sirring me all the damn day long.
                Call me Jack, dammit.
                         —Okay, Jack. Scotch, straight up.
—Three full fingers. Big old fingers. Don't be shy.
                              Hear me?
—Yes, Sir. Jack.

DOWN THE MUSIC

The first word cut off
By my mother's cough,
The first time blood ran
Staining her bottom lip
On a Florida family trip
Where my father's legs were tan
Around the gartered socks he wore
As he pulled into a convenience store
In the fizzing rain,
Knowing, physician he was,
That for her not to know the cause
Was better until we got back,
And the test tubes lined in a stack
Could diagnose the bitter music from within
He'd caught hints of in her cough so thin,
And in the strings of blood she hadn't seen
Stretched across the pillow like an anemone.

My mother was famous for dying
Her illnesses came like the red birds in the yard,
Coming and going with the seasons,
Moving with their own rhythm and reasons.

In the end she was not resistant.
A new, virulent strain had gone to work
Faster than the chemicals that were bent
On running through her lungs and chart.
She played her part.
She always said she'd be on the stage.
But it wasn't her heart.
Her passion held until the end.
It was a lack of wind.
"People just don't die of such a thing anymore.
"It's preposterous," she said.
Four months later, bald and pale, she was dead
Of a gunshot wound to the head.
My father found the wig in the sink.

WAY OF THE DOLPHINS

Those emblems of faith along your arms
Color my see thing, and your partner
Passes over your section of the allotted space.
You gave all you had for this metal
Taste of failure. The firehouse there

Is on code blue and the pumps are primed
Regarding municipal drinking fountains someone
Places in hapless places you chance upon

As a reward. You've been apt to confuse things,
But your sisters and brothers need you
To lend a hand. We're mostly on your side. Mostly.
Don't get us wrong. Just when you're sick and all—

Well, all we can do is
            Thank you for listening.

4/7 PSALM

You ordered me taken by force,
O Spirit of the Universe. The mercies of the wicked
Sucked me deep into a metal shaving mirror.
My life underground is ether and acetylene
& sparks off untouchable women in the street.
Cast your light in this labyrinth of building longing.
These rare times you allow me to surface
As ink in a notebook not likely to be read
Is spent at this table trying to get
Out brown stains from a monogrammed pillowcase.
Lo, I am drawn to what is wicked—the dark, shining
Eyes of charismatic friends.
O for some light through this cracked blue ice,
Damn the bright husky eyes that take in both everything
And nothing. My hand can't yet seem to wave
Good-bye to the Righteous, nor can it quit shaking
This Devil's pair of carved bone dice.

JUST OFF THE COAST

From her quill flows a reluctant yellow flower—
A diverse intelligence, ultra-violet, hand-pressed, intaglio prints.
Three pumpkins on a bale are an omen to her,
But they might, plainly, speak differently to you.
Still, the flowers count in this silence, outside
The bodega, open and there for her gaze. What remains

To allow? Hardbodies on television.
Her quill is subjected to sweeping floors.
It is a quill, not a spirit's broom for pay. She has other designs—
To avoid the needlework that stole seven years
Apprenticeship in death. Doves on the power line,
Clasping transmissions, coo pale coo pale

Coo pale back to one another above the white wheat.
This surface is not as hard as she can make them.
It is a matter of her own well being.
It has, she suspects, dark, warm coves of yesterday
And today pressed between its pages of pure luck.
A windy being, she, funneling the dry leaves

Long enough to signal direct dilation to someone
She's never met but talks to in her slumbers
When the blinds are open and she dozes off—
Some other half of her; gently, now, gently. She
Sends out blurred fragments of agency, pastel fingerprints.
Maybe not in this drab dress, but who knows? Find me.

OF BEING IN THE TRUTH

It's hard to wear this white jacket
Whether or not it induces pleasure.
The weather is an enlargement of your eye.
Ancestors stray, alone conspiring.

Rack them up, my man. The game
Of faces stirs the kettle's cloudy delusions.
Please speak of the place we share. If you
Think it's brown, who's to say it's not?

And the circling Sun, and the darkening ethos
Have wanted to talk to you one-to-one,
But you fear the you of you would be wiped out.
The Moon is crazy. Slovenly bitch.

BLACK RINGLETS

I saw your name in a decoy notebook.
People shred all of us that belongs—

An earwax ghost remembered what you did
Alone with the pages in heathen forget-me-nots.

The trading bell has grown over with Spanish moss.
They've never heard of putting sugar in your tonic here.
Even your hair is terribly sensitive.

People ask what I think of those times
All the time,

                    I won't say, but you still lend
Lies to me to answer the echoes.

The innards of this drone
Coil you back hometown, mother tongue,
And you are sitting there in your teeth
About to get trapped in a box
Someone has trapped a lotta folks in.

Tight, snug as rounds in chambers, the
More you struggle, you'll get the picture.
On the Dead Sea we sunned and
Darkened our oiled bodies.

And all this will get straightened out somehow.
Someday, by Somebody,
But only long after the class has ended.
The lucky few get there only one by one.

The hammer is missing a claw tooth,
But not a word blotted, each driven home.
Right. We'll have to come out around four and wash
The sand off our feet before we come in.
And then go off
            Alone
                  Into our darknesses
Private and Various.

STAGE OF SORTS

Grief in lowercase would drink
You away this morning when the bar opens
Up the street where you might meet
Some unaccounted swain from your history.

All sorts of red flags go up. Jeez.
Waving good-bye in hazy afternoon.
Soon may come the ring—soon you may sing
On the bridge before the Great Congregation.

Longing helps you figure what you need, for real.
But so does suffering get-what-you-pay-for wisdom.
The books tell us this. Blah. Blah to the books.
Your wrist keeps your hand attached

To the rest of your nice body, not
For easy exits and departures, before the scene
Ends with a player balled in a cold pool of blood.
Ball up this page. Toss it into the darkening wings.

DOUBLE EGYPT SURPRISE

Father, old, this virgin snow
Gets trampled by and by.

Cow paddies, mid-spring mushrooms
We ate, father, and now can see.

How hard it is for the husband to be,
Caught not in Nature's net

But in subtle laws of "Man's" devising—
Such ideas light up her first cherry dawn.

I don't like this one very much,
But some of the others are pretty okay.

Trust, after 2 AM on a cool June night
You'll be glad to have them safe in bed.

LONGER THAN YOUR SLEEVE

They usually make it look like an accident.
Let go. Always monkeying
In God's rafters. As you gloss
Stars, lovers are busy building walls.
I like eating cake too. The new
Turning of time you've been thinking about—
But I'm a "show-me kind of guy." Old men's
White hair regaining its youthful color
And luster. The new laws
Provide we must purify the seas,
Starting with the seas themselves,
And working back up the estuaries,
Foot-by-foot up the rivers where someone
Quite like you squats in a dunce cap.

3/28 POEM

Meet me under the dumbass sconces
Catercorner beneath the blondest atmosphere—
Here and now, dissolving again
Down industrial streets to the proofing grounds.

I lied and yet I tried to learn to draw chalk
Shop window mannequins in the dead streetlight glow
Where winter hides her truth in the lake

Under ice where you get chills watching

Skaters cutting sleek infinities into a gray sheet,

And there's the perfection of glass figurines
Who repeat to themselves that they will not break
No matter
        What
            This time.

VARIABLES

Color comes through your mute eye—
Not in, what you see,
Hard to hear the tonic chord
In pure cacophony.

Older, day by day,
Lost lessons time bought,
You made the F car.
But your black silk tie got caught.

Peopled all around you,
Must they? And how can you tell
If this woolen life's a sham?
Are the batteries the vendors sell

Duds dead in a day?
And midway between stops, a woman
Recites the "Woman at the Well"—
Letting the sick speak their own way.

But who are the sick? Who's "Okay"?,
Junk cars, untailored suits, T-shirts,
Graffiti wires, your spine hurts
From your boots up. No home to not go back.

ANOTHER STONE

Are your hands strong enough to wash away
These troubles you've carried around today,
In one form or another,
Though each different from the other?
When the pricks you kick at every turn
Confound raw skin and bone
Guiding you as you seek to earn
The Dubious Right to heft the stone.
The magic of it takes a while.
You work with chisel, plumb, and file;
Then cuffed, it is put on
In the baked, brown field at dawn.
The crop stood stubble brown,
And down came the rain. They scattered 'round,
Sweet as the mandolin's thin strain and strum.
It drowned out the diminished clouds; the blackbirds reeled.
Was there ever a scarecrow that was healed?

DUMB

Some something stole my tongue.
Once it spoke its mind,
But the sense it had sung,
Is now hard to find.

Dead men, on the gallows,
Hear tunes run through fear—
The dropping-floor, a harmony follows
Eternal in the ear.

THE HYMN WARD

Long lost, they're swept away,
But they get an hour to sing
A different leaf each day,
Called together by the bells' ring.

Such sweet traffic outside the wall—
The screech and honk of the Bridegroom's Bride,
In haste, and the people seldom call
The ones who live inside.

They are washed clean of their names.
They are scrubbed of old dreams.
And they are taught to play games
To teach them be from seems.

THE RUINS

Crumble to the touch,
         Pine slats and plaster, living grass run wild
Within the foundation. If the children peer,

Toe at the ledge of the dead leaves, it is a curious anguish
        Spreads through them.
The laughing spirits hiss like a kettle
    Through the remnants of basement windows.
        And your bird-on-a-wire private messages
Echo back from us to you.   A bird laid blue spotted eggs

    Nestled in a nook of the spilled chimney bricks.   In time
They fly off, populate other people's dreams

    With frisson flashes.   The house is host
To receiving and sending denizens. Pictures here come out blank as ether,
And it is possible none of this, or us, exist, at least on this plane.

Or so on green days say the children of the instep arch.
    The moss-covered sofa is more part of Mother Earth

Than the realm of Heaven. Rusty springs strung around with ivy and vine.
    And she heard something of you, as you engaged her, knowingly
Or not. She said you were on a bus headed someplace where you
        Had doubts you would belong for long, after the eggshells

Had all been tread upon. And the rainbow you saw with your eyes
    Dreamy and half-closed was sent by someone else. Not to take credit
Where no credit is due. Someone is sweet on you.
    She dubbed you 'Lucky' for future transmissions.

Take it from me, that's a good sign the universe is paying some attention
to you.

We hope you are well, and that we can get together sometime.
We'll meet at the station. I will be in blue with a folded tabloid.

      It is their consensus that if you are willing to wear red,
By all means do. It would be fetching,
    And it is true, as all edicts issued from the laughing room are
(Not a word of this to anyone)
Like pennies pitched at a lonesome curb
                    Where free will quietly rolls away—
    From friends above to friends below
And back again. Selah.

STRATA

The rain blows wrecking the morning
    So we stay home,
        Put off the laundromat
For yet another day.

Moods of quiet stubbornness, pay backs, pay checks,
    Squat like a boulder, a character defect,
        Fossilized feelings, a petrified stump
Stood on end, roots dissolved in dirt,

Mulch of injury, loam of loss.
    I go over the day's hours—each by each.
        Recount the skeletons, the prosthetic limbs,
Uncover pebbles and lust

In brushing the conscience clean over that really hot
        Friend of yours, Anne, I
        Met
        Secretly
        Last Thursday,

    But your hook of bone brings me back to home,
        To the Safe and Warm of pure need.

        And the hook? The hook of my Have to Have,
Reeling me back to dishes in the sink,
        The busted ceiling fan,
The space we share the love between us. That hook.
Was it fashioned, just out of curiosity,
        By nature or humankind?
The way the mysteries of the Spirit of the Universe go on,
    I doubt if even God will ever say for sure.

YARD MAN

Picking up
        Sticks in the old lady's
    Yard
    That came down Sunday night in the wind
And drench.
    Shooka messa limbs every which way. I still don't have
No power. And there's all this gravel
        In the ditch needs shoveling.
    No one else to do it.
Old lady's son's a nut job.
    Heard he just got off the farm again.
One time I saw him eat a daffodil. A couple of them.
        Hour ago he came out
In a robe and slippers and offered me a beer. I said without looking
At him that I don't drink on the job. Bad luck
    To look crazy people in the eye. He has these clear eyes
That don't settle on you, just kinda float like he's
        In a field watching clouds pass. But the daughter—
She's another story. Nineteen or so, just back from college.
Let me tell you.

        Never so much as said boo to me.
After this I gotta put down some
        mulch round the boxwoods. Take
My own sweet time about it. Yes, Sir. My own sweet time.

THE CLOVER PATCH

Because I learned to love you
Away from the rest,
In a way neither logical nor sane,
I wondered if our love was not as good—
If it counted less.

But all that doesn't matter right now.
I want you to be happy,
If only as long as it takes
To see another shamrock pressed
Into the book you keep of wax pages.

Because when they bring you back,
You never know your name,
Or my name,
Or where you put the book of wax pages
Before you went to bed.

I want to have a shamrock ready—
A four-leafed wish to press in your palm
And get you a cup of coffee,
Talk about things you will forget you said.
Chase away the monster's blank face.

The day has come.
Knowing a new course is scheduled,
You bite your nether lip and hurl
Your paperback at the TV.
Luckless, it is handed to you

And to me, to live
With an extra, little leaf, a signal
For the benders to dip and pluck by.
"Special" they call us,
At the mercy of their pills and walls.

Administered the prep,
Faith, you go slowly under.
Your mouth opens as if to kiss.
O Faith, it will be ok.
And they roll you off to the room.

Through the back slit
Of the blue gown, I wondered at the feathers
The doctors and nurses seem to see—
Those people who know so well how
To diagnose, but so little how to cure.

The feathers they talk us into showing.
Maybe there was some cosmic down drifted
Wavering from a star or a heaven,
That we couldn't sneeze out like the healthy
Others more resistant to life.

Faith, I have been in the courtyard
An hour now. I haven't found a single shamrock.
The patch is small. I may have gotten them all.
But I will stay here looking, stay until one of the male
Nurses tells me to come inside from my cigarette.

TWO UP FROM DOG STAR

Yes, I guess you could call it a beautiful thing,
But someone always cites a problem, a tusk
That sticks out too far. Still nothing gets me
Like large, spotted cats when they are giving chase.

I have lounged the morning here, beneath the bug netting.
I had a dream a hyena ate a guide's face off (the one you like)
As he was sleeping. But awakening I was assured
Like most things in my life, it was only a dream.

You went (I was told) out early with your Hasselblad.
You have a weakness for the lake mist that time of day.
"Today in the water I thought I saw two dolphins," you said.
Someone is making a hellova racket in camp,

Like he's knocking on an oil drum with a length of pipe.
And in this rotating democracy it is my turn to cook lunch,
Then make rounds as guide, chance the snaky green tufts
Towards grazing gazelle. I'm ready. Just say the word.

THE CORNER

Should she romanticize it, let the red rust redden—
The redness of robins, the bobbin of scarlet thread?
It is not first fear that is her failure, that can't be helped,
But the moment's memory clinching an attack.

Facing away from the routine faces
That in her fiction turn her way in secret.
She feels like a bad hand of spades, folded forever.
O the horror she will faint into a stranger's arms

And "come to" in a kitchen in a distant city,
Cooking for the man who happened to be standing there
When everything went black and the gnats
Of destiny swam in her shadow.

BOUNCING OFF CLOUDS (TECHNIQUE 14-B)

An injection can make for a fraud, but the signals
Clear as crystal and certain mushrooms keep a handful
Of us in pods. Rules of the Road: No Proper Names,
No Street Names, and Minimal Post King James Verbal Activity.
Alas for all you know, you could be stuck in some rushes somewhere.
Our love has proven a rowboat without paddles.

Yes, sometimes I thinketh so myself. And the eighth nerve
Of the cranium…scratch that diction, is enlarged in dolphins.
This worketh for signals and echolocation (think of the readership lost).
A long spell you durst waited on the bench on the promenade, only
To see them coming anon as I was going.
I was too shy for mouth words. I flushed, turned the other way.

Yet I was visited by real women all hours of the night,
Buzzing at 5 a.m. back in the days before my roof blew off.
Body language is really a primitive way of sending out.
We, or is it God, have preserved this Black Box.
If only they would let us play it back the way we know how.
Rewind, Stop, Play: The rest is history, eh?

FOR "EMILY GLASS," WHEREVER I MAY...

But this is the way I guess it has fallen out—
None of that wedding cake icing and rummaging
Through the junkyard of shoe closets. She is here—
Aura going like a flame from orange to blue to yellow.
Someone asked if you had finished putting on the addition.
He didn't know you live by bivouac in the park. He must
He must He must have confused you with some former husband
Emily had before the gauze was taken off.

I liked sleeping under the stars with Emily Glass.
But that army of luck's light went AWOL when Emily ditched me.

I don't look like much now, so the layovers
At Greyhound terminals aren't bogged down with bus talk.
Last trip, they lost, or I lost, most of my possessions.
Bus #46, bound for Florida, slipped out of the lot while I was still
Wolfing down a burger and onion rings.
Nowadays, I feel more like a bricklayer than anything else.
I have a foreboding I should take up work with my hands.
And with this gray coming in, people keep
Referring to me as "Sir." Only I don't know if they mean it
Or are mocking me. All amounts to the same thing.
So, not yet forty, I am going in the crazy circles
Never entering her building and never getting off.
I go round till the doorman at Emily's building spies
Me in the rotating door, getting my cheap thrills,
He tells me, straight faced, "All right, Mac, that's enough."

SCRIBE

You played roles with that certain someone today?
And swiped slices of jade from a Chinese garden? Yes. I see.
Everything connects. The shield of a knight in yellow stockings—
He was too fine. Saw the future. Coming anon in a jumble of letters.

Pleasure, yes, go on, please, that is what you say you felt at first,
The bones of your body shifting lightly under your skin,
The gravity of three-cherries to a stem red and royal blue plumes
Filtering through the stained glass of memory.

And have you had any dreams? Yes, it was only
The beginning of something that would swallow you up, I see,
But more about what you felt. You felt grace? Scarlet in your cheek?
And opening this page you find someone wearing a mustache.

Twins are reunited in these cases. Your necklace drags across the page.
Music now to give a mood to the past now concerns us.
It's not in the job description to decipher these references.
Listen. Hey, be glad that someone cares for your dreams so much.

SECOND GUESSING

Who in her school of law heeds proper deportment
When the serum of truth gathers and drips from her lips?
Just how to deal with a lower east side woman in the midst
Of her solipsistic mouthings is not clear to the other associates.

The first time the nightswimming club saw her naked
She was self-conscious of private parts exposed.
In the bulbs of blacklight darkling unreal glow
Regulars peeled oranges and admired her gazelle lines.

Stung, several times, she couldn't keep count.
"That is just a normal puffing around the eyes from crying
Have you talked to the police?" She learned not to go
Anywhere near a certain Japanese paper lantern factory again.

Her hope was pinned to him who tried to stop the "General Games,"
A fool's card in his bare, unsandaled Joshua feet
Tramping midtown, dancing to keep "a polished maiden intact."
He saw her face down on the copy machine in flashes and spells.

There was the cooked smack of the past, the parting throes,
The "magical thinking" carried in common. Shifting in her sheer dress,
Centerless, her heart was a green onion ungrounded. Trick is
You got to know when to stop peeling if you want something left.

SMALL CRAFT ADVISORY

A smoke burns quietly in the ashtray,
And yesterday displaced a mood somewhere—distance,
My disorder says "Hello" and flushes the chum trap.

Skirmish lines, infrared, random speech acts add
Color to the hot wire—closing the body's eyes to it.
The game is played with brown money and chloroform.

Hap configures pulling a cunning tooth
In the chalice line: Please, brother me out of this distance.
Yesterday's green cherries, bothered and halved, stem

End tongue-tied. Now her shadows are but muted grapes,
Comprising an afternoon's anomie. Feathers, Father, give
Feathers to the doppels, so we can tell us apart.

DURING YOGA CLASS

Now I am
A little older,
Like a failed Houdini,
Who hasn't figured
His way out of these cuffs
That bind me
From passing this note
To you.

Rain and the curtain
Wavers like a wraith
Neglected, and your hair
And eyes and smile and patterned
Shirt you bought
(I heard you say)
On Court Street
Distract me from my pose.

Your body's lines—
A sinuous thrill
Even when I'm upside down.
I don't know why I hurt
Inside the way I do, and
I can't stand much longer
On my head without
Your hands to spot me.

THE RESISTANCE

I once thought him a very tweaked woman, but now I know
By the poisonous heft he presses his pen into me that I was
Formed letter by letter by a male specie, and one somewhat
Petulant the way he stalls his bird-track cursive when he
Wants to find the right word to spice me up, to give me that
Little something extra he feels he brings into the circle.   .
It's ridiculous—I can almost see him bite his lip and sigh.
But word is he's plum out of doggerel to spout.
I'm thinking of maybe doing something, going to Bermuda.
Lord knows I need a break from his stuffy little loft space.
And no lovers in the offing. It's been a bad bull of a love year.
You would think he was holding out for Aphrodite herself.
For love has shunned him, denied him her exquisite favors.
I could go on forever about this soulless soul
Who has guided me into one majorly weedy, snaky harbor—
The one who has left me at the wheel to shake us loose.
To think, in another life I could have been a greeting card
Sweet and banal, mass-produced in all my pastel glory,
And here I am, my maker asleep. In this darkness I press on.

THE CONFLICT

I am confused, as a poem, as to which sex I am.
Am I tall, striking, dimpled, dumpy, brawny, flat-chested?
Do I strike people, generally speaking, in a winsome fashion?
Am I the product of a Saturday night accident?
Are there people who can answer back? Can you?
Do my friends really see me really or just skim me over?
Do I even have friends? Do they too ask such questions?
How did I learn to speak for me, myself?
Am I an absence or a presence? Am I even a body?
Or am I a brown moth batting the window screen at night?
I fear there are deep, yet not fatal, flaws in my character
That people would have me talk more about.
I cannot distinguish a thought from an emotion.
Does one come from the body—the gut, the heart,
Some visceral seat or plexus? The other from my head?
Do I as a poem have right to make claim of having
Such things as a heart or a head or, say, an abscessed molar?
I seem guided by some agency, quite singular,
Which uses me to escape from his or her sundry fears.
I have grown tired of being used as such. Where's
The payback? If you see who or whatever made me,
Tell it, or him, or her I will no longer play the pawn.

SUMMER COTTAGE

Your long hair streams from the shower, tresses
Disheveled. You go for the same relic of a red dress.
O your hair, after so many years, each hair numbered,
Each brow hair, even the thinnest is counted.

And for years now we've come here, with summer and all
Parting us at the seams, like froth vanishing into the tide.
At least we've had a thatch roof over our heads all these years.
Strange, we now never need to speak. But last

Night we talked. (I can't tell who's doing the talking
Anymore.) But I think I heard that you say you hold it dear
That everything that is going to happen has happened
Already, and life is one long movie trailer we must live out.

And who am I to argue. I'm not what you call the thinking type.
I went out and got the grill going, got a nice even heat.
Those rib eyes had my name on them and the eggplant
You got me to pick up at the store came out to perfection.

HELLO

Hello
Whoever you were
This evening on Orange Street,
Who held me, loosely
Fastened, three or four blocks
To the earth feeling nervous
And nearly handsome
Every third odd step. Then she,
The mother of all abstraction,
Took me hand in hand
In her deathly white gloves
And escorted me in
Inscrutable silence
Towards our usual place—
Perennial companion who knows
Not jealousy, but bemusement.
"Ah, my dear, you've been
Tarrying again. Did you think
Her pretty? Did you suppose
Something could have come of it?"
And imperceptibly we go
Up the stairs, her dress rustling,
Trailing behind us,
To the ballroom the lonely
Non-existent go to dance
The gay, old waltzes, while
The ghostly chaperones talk
Of Calvin Coolidge
And toast each other's empty
Crystal glasses.

SUBJECT BODY

SUBJECT BODY

1

A subject body was he and he was Subject Body.
He was born and things happened. He piled things
In places. People unpiled them.
But also good things sometimes. Knuckle deep in candy corn,
He'd have polished off the whole. Me am lithper;
No, me am lisper. Subject Body the Younger stepped
On the heroic scale and measured up not. Doctors made
Special shoes so the little fellow who tippled
Could stride. Unga! Me am lithper. And the rides
Spun sometimes too fast. And legs smooth
Were of ladies. And the grown ups swung their arms just so.

2

Sylvan was young Subject Body, chubfishing.
All in a flow of stream. He turned slates upways
For lanky baitworms; crickets whirred the young master to sleep,
Hoppers spat. Dough ball, pork rind,
Blue spoon, and bucktail. Young Subject Body sank
Barefoot through silt, and he prayed
The monster should not choose him, for he was small and mostly bones.
And alone in a shale bed, shadowed by a cold mountain, he once saw
A little trout and loved it. And he threw a clod in to show his love.
And when the ripples had all rung out,
Flat in the glass he spied a face. And it was his very own.

3

"Your mummy's not your mummy," said Chip the Boy
Who lived across the street. Words were exchanged.
Little Subject Body came home covered in noseblood.
And so many tears he couldn't cry out them fast enough. And who
Was this woman who wiped the snot from his face?
Something in him tore itself away and rattled, but not too loudly.
Not loud enough for anyone to hear.
Besides there was still summer left, and sometimes birds
And sometimes colored stones. And one evening at a cookout,
A man he'd never seen before laughed
And laughed and picked him up and called him son.

57

4

Hello golden rule and the redwhiteandblue flag he pledged to,
And the candy he lifted from the shop. Head on his desk, he pondered
Chalk dust and cursive and the ankles of a young crush.
Yes. Subject Body was mostly in Mrs. Tennant's homeroom, but Africa
Was calling, and off he went, lamenting as he waved good-bye.
Africa was calling, The King required the young Subject's service.
The Fastest Boy Runner In The World, whose once lame feet
Had outstripped during recess all others.
Hi there through keyholes. He goes on, through fog in the Blue Ridge
Where Subject Body was sweet to bugs. Keening the way the summers say
"Strumming guitars have gone on holiday, lonely lad. Follow me."

5

Seldom when a wink disturbed his faze
Would Subject right the wrong. Sensitive
Subject was, but not one to find them by.
He threw games, jostled pieces, bumped
A girl on the bus for all his temper.
He sulked off to the prickly bushes
When all the others were playing dodge,
Pieced things like long hair in his mind,
Troubled the already troubled waters—
And the berries he would die if he ate
Grew dark like blondes in the sun.

6

A lithe young Body took to heart
Not to hold his face like that, or it might get stuck.
Compressed young Body foresaw the present—
Where visitation was first felt, cut wood and struck
Camp. Subject Body's misunderstanding
Exceeded his small compass, with which
He etched obscenity into the desk.
And balls of dust crept "Hello" with their smiles.
Young Body served, he told himself, a faction injured
Who saw God in the eyes of scattered birds—
Out of bounds already, ever opening wider.

7

In class mostly friends with his desk, imaginative boy.
He'd made jet controls there and engaged
Fellow pupils in combat. An ace at eight.
In church heaven wore away. Mossy patchwork
And wet sticks spoke close to his heart—
Those with an ear could hear. He must have fashioned
The black creek and the crayfish dodging
Tail-backward his lifting of them from their stones.
Alone, young Subject was such always engaged.
Supper was laughter and butter beans,
But the dark was in Subject's blood: lost summer daze.

8

Pebble by pebble he came to see
His own developing, as he became more
Of a young Subject Body. He weighed in
At gym and came up light
For his height and bodily girth. Spoon
By spoon, the subject was helped to ice cream
And what might fatten him to normal measurements.
Finally, he was right, and weighed in proper.
He fit the chart and no more blood work was required.
That was for later when young Subject Body's life
Fell into final and lovely pieces.

9

Fossils, petrified wood, rattlesnake tails—
Subject Body's backyard was a digging through the past,
And fangs of the slider he invented inside.
Subject Body presented to the eternal, but
Without glasses everything was a Chinese blur.
Games sometimes he played with the other kids—
Roughed up with grass stains on his knees,
He mostly tucked himself in safe while others
Became dirty names and plots to get even—
His one gift, to put a red arrow every time
Into the black cross of the sun's yellow eye.

10

Subject Body pressed against a wall
Spat back in a bully's face. He was propped
Along the lacquered black bench of the Principal.
"Now what's this I hear. What's this I hear?"
Subject felt like a flag dropped and burnt,
All over a fight over a Crush. Subject spat a tooth
Loose to his surprise. Sunrise at morning—
Somewhere he always kept changing.
Mother vacuumed pennies into the machine,
And young Subject palmed a bloody incisor
Off and away from Heaven's sight.

11

Abject in company, when guests showed their faces
Young Subject felt surmounted. One had a Hello Bird
Perched in its mouth cage. Seeds he ate were confessed.
And then they got a Game going,
And young Subject was picked for once—the Body
In the field was Taking Orders: need to know only.
And far in right field, Subject Body caught a Pop Fly.
Much he pleaded cheers from his very own team,
But it made for division, as the Book said it ought.
The heart of the young Body went out
To his True Sister and their sickness of the blood.

12

Off to Church went the Subject each Sunday morn—
Church was coat and tie and the Preacher who strummed
Songs echoing through the Stone Walls. Subject jestered
His Calling. God was long shafted arrows with fletchings
Of feathers. But he heard from the purple Pulpit
The words, words, words of Talbot's Dreaming Dress.
Crush…Strike three. The Lord was stand up, kneel.
Imagined attackers he and his bow would fend off—
And the go-in hymn and the go-out hymn: Sleepy
Sounds of droning words and answers
But none of them came Alive again, not one, not yet.

13

Subject Body perched out the window to see
The gray-blue smoke plume from his mouth in the dark.
He thought of all the cavities the dentist drilled. Much
Had been drilled into Subject Body. If the bit
Drew blood Subject Body would become largely
A spit in the white bowl take it like a man kind of guy.
The smoke caught in the wind, beginning a descent.
The tennis balls all went flat for bongs.
With his new sexual nexus came a stutter.
His glands gave him a tick but no tock.
He reached out, rode limbs to the proofed ground.

14

Smut mags, cigs, and sneaking old whiskey
From the cabinet, new positions on the shower tile.
Subject had erased Lennon's face and drawn his own.
Verily a collage of what he shouldn't most do.
And the Family far away, dressed up Subject,
But Subject insisted on a floppy leather hat.
Sleds were no longer what got his rocks off.
Prurient Subject Body was a body of the senses—
Young and doped out methadrine river boy
Who was having kicks, Fun for the first time.
One night as he crept in, he heard his father crying.

15

Subject Body perked up at certain Sounds
Like Rain at Random, a Pattern sought he—
A Scheme, a grande Life View, but all he had was a Bag
Of Glue into which he sought Consolation, model Glue
For the Ship he was building in his Head.
This piece went Here, that one There, but the stuff
Got Stuck in his hair, and he Sailed on Lost
To the Stars' dead reckoning; Life was Cloudy
And the Rain lied as it Fell—Music.
Gold rivulets Shone in Streetlight
At Night walking to the place called Home.

16

His Father told him not to Pick at the Bites,
But Subject Body Picked anyways. A glow
Of Red Flooded his very Skin, Pumped from his Heart—
Lovely Red. And once, Carving a Lure,
He Stuck his Palm Good. So faint did he.
He was Rushed to the Emergency Room.
Hours passed Stitch after Stitch.
He went under spinning, counting back from a hundred
The Masked Men's faces. He seemed Stuck
In a Huge Clock that went tick, tick, tick—
But never Tock....despite his Pleading, never Tock.

17

Sped through a Montage Machine, Subject lost his Grip.
He bedded Girls in the same Spot. It was Mossy
Golf Course Hole #9. Sports? No. Friends? Few.
But some Stuck Up for him when he was Reassigned
According to the Ledger of the Lost. Kegs and Pumps, Red
Plastic cups, Strumming Girls' Hearts—Away.
Strands of Pearl and Hunting Deer—Green Air
Of the Season, turning soon Sweet on Him Again
And his 10-sized feet. Mother and Father—
So far away he couldn't Catch the Flies in the Field Forever.
Ever Given to him who Knew not How to Receive.

18

Busted for Substance, heads Subject Body
To the Rehab Center. So went Youth,
Hello to Peeling his Feelings, nothing, Numb—
Shame fell, a Pall, on Subject's Self.
Apple juice in little paper cups, playing Spades.
Those who know, know, and the Group
Where Others Broke Down and Spilt Things.
Subject in Pain—his Future Falling Faster
Down through the Box of Music. Felt
The Subject like a Russian Doll, an Onion
Each taking his turn to Peel. No shoes allowed.

19

Subject Body indexed things: Green feathers
Plucked from a noble Bird of Flight, were dyed green
In a Funk of his Misgivings. Sense was fallen,
Burst like Grapeshot. The Bod Eat and Drink and Sleep.
Acceptance is the touchstone of the Mansion
Where the windows spangle Stars frosty Morns.
He seeks a bed to plant his Seed by,
But the New Moon was up to Tricks again.
So Subject Body Wheeled through the yellow Corn—
The tassles and husks, Green for his Grandpa,
The Scarecrow who Knows of what he Speaks.

20

To Rule or to Serve: the Subject Dilated
'Tween his moral Ears. What are the Stakes? Any?
He wooed them Quiet as an Adjunct; Hellish
Brain depicting 'Tween Abstract Entities.
His Guitar His Bath of Blood—a Ghost he Chose.
Feeling for a Chinese Lamp—jingle of tiny bells.
A wan woman crossed, beers to forget by.
Dark hair and long lashes, he consumed.
And lonely on God's sofa, he jettisoned his Part.
The speaking parts were Dead, Remiss.
And where he goes God only Guesses.

21

Day Wine streams from the Sky. Perfect Hands
Catch it in a Lead Crystal Cup. Subject Body
Holds everyone for Questioning—Ahem.
A delirious girl watches everything from her Bath.
None of this, she knows, was supposed to be.
The whole Charade makes her Think, She Loves
Subject Body, but not his Rubber Ball. He is
A Harp in the Night of her Drifting—
But the Math Never works out Right.
The Elegance is like a Set of Tarnished Plates
Sent off to France, She sends her Love…XXX.

22

In a Drab Dress pressed beneath a Cloudy Day,
Subject Body thought of her in italics when he did.
The Bod is Helpless to Fix her in his Male Gaze,
Until he first saw the Vertical Stitches on her Wrist
Something in his Teeth Hurt, He put down the Nikon.
Later he Told her he wanted them to Live under Thatch—
For nothing to ever hurt or wound her again.
He would Square her Circle with his Warm Hands.
And to his Surprise she took him up on it.
The Greatest Gift Working the Garden Outside
And Seeing her Chin at the Window Peering out.

23

Thud for Days, Netted Flesh, little Barbs—
The World Outside a who's who of Divers Down.
Scavenged and Salvaged—Bits of Love Recalled.
Now all felt like Bleached Birds, of Teeth and Bone.
God must have been Tending Things. Subject Body
Wove his Fingers, Coined Phrases
That rung around his Darkened Dragon Aura.
And all around people Spread in his Path—
Seeing the Numbers on his jersey, Turn Away
Subject Body…Turn, Turn. Away.
Away Subject Body…Away, Away, Away.

24

If it should Lift—this Gray Limestone Affair,
Would Friend or Lover Slip a Finger through the Catch
And Throw it Open all the Way? To Dance Death's Dance?
Subject Body Craves Bright Days. He and She
Would Slip Away, Breathless, Around their Mortgaged Houses
They would Go to Come to Life Again, in
One Another's Domestic Arms. She in her Gown,
Thick Grow the Mosses where once they had lain,
And the porcelain figurines on the mantel.
So Many mansions, for that's as it was writ.
Look! Her hand! The Fingers Moved!

25

A Hurricane was in town which God Sent
To help Subject Body get some Decent Sleep.
Lithe Lines to the Powers that Be. Subject B. was
A Police Officer, you see; and went on Talking—
Kaleidoscope in Hand—without Moving his Lips.
"IF YOU WANT HERE IT IS COME AND GET."
He Triangulated Lines of Transmission.
Else he'd be out Washing Down Cheap Lager
And Pills at Night to put the Wolves to Sleep.
Thank God for the other Lobsters in the Pot
Who kept Pulling him Back for his Own Good.

26

Why with All the Fear and Trembling?
The Body had Met a Born-Again Explained
Him to His Knees. Only it wasn't Right he Knew
To feign Handling Serpents to Get Her
In the Sack. But once he Started, Something
Cusped him Angel-like and Held his Writhing.
Subject Body Despaired he'd Pissed off the Lord,
But it was Max, her Ex, Breaking Bad on Him.
"I Give!" Subject said, "I Give! She's Yours"
Released, Subject Body Sank into a Spell—Cool Hands
Of Mary in the Dark—Solace Never Known.

27

Subject's Glorious Body Suffered Envy for not "Making It"
Enough, and Weak-Kneed, he Essayed
Not to Dwell in Subways at long-lashed faces and Knockers
That made Subject want to Sign-Up at the Gym.
But that just wasn't him. If they could only see—If Only.
But then Again they might run.
Telepathic Peaks and Troughs…Touch your Neck, And Again.
Mr. Strangedays Zooming in on Private Thoughts.
No. That was Just In Her Mind and She's Hungry.
"I'll Have to do the Fake Stop Thing to See if He Bites.
Shame. He has Very Beautiful Eyes."

28

The Subject was Spread-Eagle. He had been fixed.
Blurred whizzed literal translations of Catullus:
They were replaced by nifty versions like
Baneberries strewn in a bastardized Purple Field.
He had a Greek teacher made of Straw and Jam
Who kept a 9mm Browning under his buckwheat pillow.
Point is, Much of what Subject Body could Allow
Went un-expurgated before he said it out.
There were blondes, and others never
Sampled, though the sadder Lasses said, "Hello."
He shouldn't complain. Watson & Crick said so.

29

All Broke Up Inside—Like Most of Us…Subject Body's
Delicate Parts Rattled—When he was Shook.
He Prayed…Some Days; then Cursed the Light
Tucked in a Ball through Lonely Nights.
Subject had been Trained to Fight, but not Shadows
And the Blank Things he was in the Small Hours.
Nothing to Swing at—Blank Blank Blanks to Fill in.
Bells Tolled and in Dreams went on Blinking.
There came Signs—Of his nearly Giving in.
Bottles of Pills Winking above the Sink.
"Wink Back, Subject. Someone Loves You."

30

A Big Fever Hit—Knocked the O.K.
I.Q. Possessed of Subject Body Down to that
Of a Squirrel. No One knew if he'd Keep
Playing with his Lips and Rubber Balls, Like one
Who Longs to Stroke Felt. Subject Body Touched
The Mirror, and Shocked, Stepped Back.
But had his Synapses been Fried?
Aside from Bi-Polar One, this was a New Thing.
People found to Get Along with him was Easier,
But like a New Season the Cooling Came,
And Feathers Rose Over the Darkening Bay.

31

Once, the Book said that Subject—Had a Center.
No More. His Head Cleans Clear with—Space.
A Vacuum his Volatile Voltaire Hands to move through
(little case) with fingers handling Antimatter.
At Sunset Subject was on a solipsistic Quest.
Like an anti-hero, he must have gone West to Catch Fire.
He dowsed out—the personal self; for Self-Echoes
And Messianic through they gainsay, and go
Tar and Feathered back East to catch his breath
His Insurance would cover, that was Tiresias.
Blood he opened a vein in a Roman Tub: Love.

32

Some Books, departed ex-friends, were Poison—
Their gaudy caws, the condescension of their Tone.
Realizing a remark was a Cut, a mental Dig.
Who knows why? Subject Body was not Nice
And Suave went along turning on Salamanders,
Cantering on a lovely horse and expectorating.
These are not the laws of a landed gentry, he would claim
As water rolled and tumbled over freedom falls.
And without the odds of freedom falls
Subject Body's spinning body would be all money,
Laid on a barrel, by voices that kill.

33

Subject Body Sees—Asian Gods Wink Zero,
Points to a Rice-Walled Mansion to be Filled.
Subject meditating says, "Don't Stare." He knows Stations
Laden with White Noise, Static lonely as Bones.
He turned She and thought on Things, Turned
'Round in a Blindfolded Kid's Game, Turned around
In his Astral Seat and was Lost. The game of Stars
Eaten through like Silk and Verbiage.
Still-frames of the People he Met and Forgot.
He Trades in Love Lost; Pure Surplus—
A pink Moth batting at the Window Screen.

34

Subject Bubble digs some happy breeder gone—
He needs to Chest It, Subvert the candy dark Triangle,
New life Drowning despite Lovely Lanes of Rain—
News of such old Memories dry him Humming Dry.
Around the vertiginous Wax, Waves Pull at us.
The Grayhound works its way home, the Scottish
Burns backwards, Meanwhile the Mottled Sun
Burns what it is I meant in spots of backward certain
Fireman Dog Flush for Other Lover's Safety—
Running hard the unspoken path, the words:
We share things, see, Beyond the Borders.

35

The Story in the Hand Shatters like Glass—
Wine in Subject Body's half-empty, half-full Life.
He is Thinking the Words from her Mouth.
She is Dreaming the Thoughts of his Night.
Bend, he does, Beneath the Weight of her Step.
Bends, he gets, Rising through her Depths.
She Polices the Suburbs of his Farthest Fancy.
Nothing is Noted, Told Outright or Uttered.
The Decoys Bob in the Tide of Shared Blood—
All Our Blood. A Stranger's Gears Mesh
With Our Deeper Dream, Our Deeper Love.

36

Just some Pills is all it took to Chill him Out—
The Landscape of his Room went Rightsideup,
Ducks Dove, Pigeons Scattered at his Feet.
The Manhattan Skyline made him less Dizzyheaded,
And the East River Ran more Green than Silt.
Still, no Quick Lovers in the Offing. And It Was Good.
He needed some Time to Get it Together
Before he was Prepared to Give his Location Away.
He ordered a slice, Gave a dollar to Someone in Need.
He Kept up with What Needed Keeping Up With.
He Watched the News. Hope was in the Trees.

37

Love you Later—Loved you Better.
Subject Body made Stars of Black Ink.
Nobody Sends Letters anymore—sentiment
Excised, but Telling is an Act Itself.
He lay on his Futon Folded up Again,
Wanting Water Wanting Water Again—
And what She might do Beside him.
Lonely went cross and Lovely numb.
Dozed off, saw Himself in a Cowl,
Working Silence into her Heart, Giving
Back—what he had taken.

38

Rooted in Rood—Monk's hood Scowls.
Where have they Fled? One took her Glasses off
And was even More Pretty for a Dazed Hour.
She Glazed the Winter Window—at odds with
Itself with all its Peopling Tendencies,
Who have been Pegged and Loitered in the State.
Subject Body wonders—if I was a Girl—
Shedding cheer with his Left Chromosome.
He scored the pills of Soothing, and took up
Gardening in the wee hours, when the seeds
Rooted spilt from his long black wings.

39

In the Depth of the Subway Boundaries Blur and Merge—
Mind Merges. I unto you—Gripping the Pole,
Watch from the Tank the Speaking Tags Strumming
Us to a Destination—Squares of Sodium Light.
Faces Swim the Backstroke in Silent Geography.
The Woman's Hair next to You is Yellow
Lighted by Harm's Highlights. She Sheds Looks
Like Lotus Flowers to the Stressed-Out Jacks and Kings.
Luck, in its Distance, Stubbed Subject Body.
Sub—Sub—Stubject Body from the Moment of his Birth,
Through the Tunnel he Arrived on Schedule.

40

Diminished, Subject Body's music failed him—
Losing his Love in the Blue, the Frame's Texture:
Subject Wounded Caught Fire, but did not Show
His glow, his Heart once More than a Path—
Noble and Eight-Folded. Now was an Ember
Through the Field Folded in all its Arpeggios.
These Articles need Reading to Save Time
Of those Dressed in Hospitals, if the Rules
Permit Reading Matter When Everyone's Lights Out.
These Subjects and Sigils help get Us Outside
The Tassels that Blind Our Sight—Unseen Angels.

41

These Bodies Darkling Touching, Old Octopus
In the Timeless Flood of Ebb and Flow.
Subject, speaking from the First Persons,
Collected Starfish in the Tide. I think he liked them
For Growing Parts back as he had done.
That last woman took seven fingers in a clutch.
The Lifeguard kicked sand in his Trousers.
In the Rain without even a clue, Red in the wind
His back was on fire as he Washed the Sand Off.
And he dreamed of her heterosexual curves;
The moon offed his head like a sickle.

42

Subject Body knocked over a red glass lamp shade—
Fate scattered it. Subject Body was unkempt with Love.
And if I feel like making Rain I do it Quick I do.
And if I think like you are the one I love, I Dream
Like a startled Dog Subject Body Overflowing the Bank.
He is Seriously bolted Down, His Love Flutters
Folded on a lichen-covered Stone. She landed
On the patterned edge of a China Bowl. I
(Subject's ventriloquism) love even the bluegrass between
Her Toes, her love of fishing, or riding horseback
Always on an English saddle, or whatever.

43

Husky-Eyed, he Ran Mexican Brown up his Huffer
Just to Drown the Diagnosed Dragon. He Ran
Long blue-tied Hits with a Rubber Hose.
He Counted his Love's Body as Mary's Cup—
Used it to Milk a Brotherhood of Blood.
In school Rubber Cement got his Rocks Off.
Subject now was Ripe for a Taste,
Winding up the Hills. He said 9:00, just a taste.
And Scoring in Red Hook Projects Dangerous—
Never know Under Cover slap your Hands on the Car.
Glassine Paper Wavering Down—Cherry Blossoms.

44

Subject Body's throat was broken open
To let loose a Blackbird with yellow eyes.
Yellow there, askew, Scarlet and Blue—
Subject was color blind: Red and Green,
And he asked the Lord for Discernment
Between agencies of Government, So
He'd know Just Who Was Bound To Take Him In.
He counts less than an Outhouse in his Hometown—
The Cold trips down the Slates in the Dark.
He Grew up in Blues and Grays,
Lucky for him, Colors he Could Tell Apart.

45

Subject Body was most Himself Whizzin'
'Gainst a Young Tree. Nature Absorbed—for You and Me.
He kept an Eye Open for the Farmer's Daughter
Who might Fill his Rump with Rock Salt.
A reference lost on City Dwellers He was stalked
By the moon and the star Draco of all values known.
Impossible woman, may I have some of the tea?
And the men you go for are the stuff of Shuffled
Bishops. I play three games at a time for life,
On the ward the skinny woman knits a sweater
No one will ever wear. She seldom looks at the TV.

46

Subject Body Swallowed the Lovely Bait.
He Played Out Hard only to be Landed in the Keel.
He was Admired for the Sheen of his Silver Scales,
And Weighed for Confirmation before being Thrown
Back in the Dark Waters that had Spawned Him.
He was a Pawn of the Worms and the Weather,
Lily Pads were his Haunt, Through which Boat
Shadowed the Surface, Stirred the Long Stems.
Fishers of Men Netted Folk of the Rainy Bank,
And Red Letter Edition Ink dripped and Pooled.
Subject Body Spat Out the Inky Words.

47

Stuck in his lower Circle, Subject Body
Resists Katabasis and Apotheosis—Lest he Turn
Forever Ungrounded and Caught in the Flame
Of All the Blessed Living and Dead.
An Idea Stuck in her Head—
The Light Shining through the Dark Netting
To Keep the Swimming Bugs of Dawn Down.
He wants his Happy Back—He wants to Scrub
And be Clean and Love Each Bird and Blade
Of the Grass that Kisses—Darkening Sky.
Long Climb to the Dripping Hive.

48

Subject to Visions, Subject Helped with the Grill.
He Flipped Burgers and Wished he was Normal.
In the Coals he saw an ever Pumping Heart.
The Guests looked like Goldfish—
Bug-eyed in a Plastic Bag held Aloft.
And here he was Subject Drunk Turning Weenies.
People smiled at him a Special Smile,
Which Subject Body Deciphered in the Falling Darkness
Of Sundresses and Earrings and Unattainable Things.
But Hungry they Ate his Work
While Subject Body Watched—Like A Mad Specter.

49

Hushed in a Moving Circle, Hands in Prayer—
Subject Body Wove in the Moving Light,
Hovering Ahead in her Oriental Hair Undone.
Cut Straight Back Black. Crouched—
The Apocalyptic Tiger Held his Magic Hand
Palm to Palm as he Glided into a Half
Lotus and Wove his Novice Fingers which
She Knew Into the Pattern of a Green God.
Then the Bell Sounded, Dulled at the Final Ring—
He Pretty much wanted to Take her Home—
Climbing the Ladder into "I Do" Forever.

50

Translucent Green-Lizard Lighters are Very Fine
And Sought by Magical Thinkers,
Which Subject Body in the End of the Movie Was.
He Sought Colored Food, In Battle with Old Men
He Soaked Apricots in Salt Solution and Spit Them Out.
He Swept Spells Into the Fireplace.
He Sought the Tree of Life and Found Children
Swinging from its Branches, Making the Subject Happy.
A Heavy Smoker, he was a Shaman Making
The Air Pure by taking in its Poisons.
This One I Meant More than the Others. No Lie.

51

No Thing Clings like the Past. Subject
Body Stripped it like Bark for a Canoe,
Where they Tap the Sweet Syrup—
But to Subject Body it's all Sweet and Sour
In a City Where he Eats Only to Sustain.
What Should be Called this Life he Lives?
If Nero Rises, Subject would Open a Vein
In a Warm Tub, Like any Noble Roman.
But Only for the Ones He'd Leave Behind.
He is a Holiday Photo and a Modest Smile.
Proof, to those he knows not, He Endures.

52

Hunger for Knowledge Leads in Due Time
To Imbecility No One can Follow; Subject Body
Subjected Much to Himself was A Lake Flower
Sparkling in a Way to Drive People Mad—
Or Turn Away toward the Teacups,
Daisies and Cowbells—All a-Sway, and Spurs
(I forgot the spurs), Spinning in the Wilting Fields
Subject Wove like Flax Time for Here to There,
Dropping Boxes Marked FRAGILE on his Toe.
No where Stayed Home for Long—
Lesson Learned—He Toed the Line.

THE HIERARCHY

They think us wobbly, un-serious souls, with their yapping
Canines keeping the blind man up. The bear, Ursa Major—
Is overturning a Volkswagen to shake out a dragon.
Mr. Smith sleeps in a factory with many people under him.

Damn the Union on strike again, with their signs saying
We will produce no more psychedelic glazes unless allowed
To share in the credit of the ever-collapsing layer cake.
Our demands are simple. We will allow no concessions.

I'm back now, over your shoulder, mouth agape in the mist,
Pinching (with permission) your chamois shirt to clean off my lenses.
A professor once deemed this style of dancing too fast.
Gone, he lost his soul somewhere in L.A. writing scripts

For game shows where the losers grit their teeth
So hard the phenotype abuse of repression imprints,
After generation, into bi-polar one or two. Please, if
You care for this poem, smash the nearest glass.

DREAMS OF CURSIVE RINGLETS

With your green eyes and hands cold as strawberry daiquiris,
Love had overflowed the sidewalk like a gutter of winter rain.
And all the time, you couldn't make up your mind
About where to get coffee and eat. Tripping down McDougal,
I would point out a place: You would give me *that look.*
And I don't know myself these days, much less you—

When and if I should convey to you these said feelings
Risking maudlin looks and bumming you totally out.
Pity I don't want or need—old days we tumbled back
Blind in the grass, climbed the gray crops of rocks
Together in Central Park, where we saw a pheasant
That had no place being there, cawing its friggin' head off,

Like a shimmering, slender, color-crowned crow.
I feel like that pheasant—out of place, no longer sure
Of your love, but I have a place to crash
And a decent mojo. Still, I would like to line my walls
With cork and have pictures of everyone tacked up,
Always there when I need them, and *especially* when I don't

To give the bird to eyes bloodshot as bull's-eyes, lidless
As catfish, linger on and wink at girls (especially you) get
Cramped in the middle seat in the taxi getting a look
From the boyfriend who's a *that's my woman* jealous type.
I'd stare at you hard in a contest I couldn't win—
Your expression forever frozen, those green eyes deathly wide.

28 WILLOW STREET

The wind blows, blows away down Willow Street
All the things so long you have kept inside.
A trailing red scarf is not a hangman's noose.
The devil is not always clicking close behind

To drive you to the other side of the street.
Nor do angelic wings ruffle in the fray.
The song of the wind is a tearful and stolen rhapsody,
Louder than the harbor-bound promenade nearby.

Its voice ripples in waves your heart's sleeves
In front of houses dated on brass plaques 1858 or 1867—
With a have-seen-it-all stoicism in red brick facade
That the wind has lied to a thousand times.

Willow Street knows me, knows you, (if you dare visit),
Knows the secret of what you carry inside.
While the side streets are deathly calm,
Here whip like stray confessions
All the lost leaves back home again.

DARK CHANNELS

You speak to me though you aren't there
Or anywhere—just a voice dreaming of grassy
Glassy squares where nothing is ever wrong.
Who knows if the sky should turn green?

And strange is the postman who keeps
Delivering the same letter day to day.
"Johnny, I feel this pining away is wasted:
But for the sheen of your body in the river."

The stars came off tonight—
Like a good neighbor they put a chokehold
On a yellow dog when it attacked me
Catching iridescent blue butterflies in a mesh net.

And I've been jamming things at random—
And bleaching the colors back to heaven,
I turn them gold and silver tinsel:
Everyone included, just like the tickets say.

FRIDAY NIGHT

Friday night on evening's cusp—
Rain falling on the A/C, wind rippling
The bottom of the blind slats
Where the window is open an inch.

Now quiet a while, then a gust—
Sounds like a deck of cards
Shuffled by a budding dumbass,
Dealt out to me, the only player left.

Where are the bongs and the beer?
Friends who would always be there?
One held a full house, one two aces.
In the end it was all a bluff.

Still, everyone must be somewhere—
Married, manic, having kids, gone gay.
Listen. There is one on the sidewalk now!
I would know those footsteps anywhere!

DAYS BEFORE THE WAR

If I could tell you the bad word going around,
It would be no birthday—no cake and candles
Whispered in the half-hour after sex
When I thumb catalogs for blue water safe resort spots,
Knowing I am getting old and the blank sun
Bleaches old men in island isolation.

No blue amazon mimics back the secret
Scrawled in pen on a legal pad. *"And your
Sheepskin and your lambskin are your
Defective forms of protection."* I see you,
Back of the N train. *"Will you let me, kindly,
Sit next to me, let me, talk back to me."*

Off to the island, tangled in topographical maps, we will take
The steep ridge, stepping to our final destination.
And such slatternly beauty, I want to awaken you
To see if you are alive or a musky plastic effigy.
Life goes on, chamomile yellow and digital camouflage.
The archduke and his bride, marked and shot.

OUTSIDE

He had been inside a trance longer to commit
To memory the danger of the chosen's eyes, the nerve stems
Wired to a lurid orange dagger-like perception,
Where no one else pulls the puppet's strings.

Shy, David the assassin, shunted Good News for olden times—
Prayed for the chosen, his enemy, to drop
From an apoplexy and turn to heap of legal vegetable.
Shy David, the assassin, had barbs on his hooks.

But rarely he sent out such prayer to himself, waves
To limit the brain's trough patterns and clot the arteries.
If you would construct the Palace of Evil,
Construct it here. It is a good place to build.

SILVER TOE RING

I am are two words to begin the begin.
You are the second, la mode in white strap sandals.
Waves of froth-colored hair follow me under.
You have an intuition thing going on,
Between the falcon freed from its hoodwink
And beauty too quick, ducking into a hole.

X holds his bag over the sea cliff talus,
And to catch your talking, I lean across the room,
And we take turns taking turns taking turns talking.
I am moving toward words as para-psychological entities,
But I keep it under this, my high-grade hat.
You are more beautiful, each look you become more

Becoming or, as they say where I am from, "fetching."
And I grow old with a tooth-colored beard, grainy, photo-like.
I that age once am not now, not "fetching."
At the water fountain saw you I, bent over blindly
Sipping, and a single summer's swallow means summer is made.
You will fully "get" this on a Wednesday or a Sunday night.

Things I know I do not know say the Long Island Shore,
And please don't freak is an abrupt skitter in diction.
I write year on year piling silver scrolls—
Another shiny prop to put in the pile of glittering targets.
The "Tonight Show" is coming on.
The lengths I go to, to practice being people.

THE ONE STROKE

I see you here, yes, left of the vertical
Line drawn when it had me making a cross,
But the blue was all wrong and the sets—
Stations—crossed my mind to look at,

Like playing, mark this corner, chess against
A stop-clock shark; Now I envision—no
Feel the texture the texture of the skin,
And the rows of white teeth that are all counted.

These cheap staples better hold. When it dries
It gets drum tight, this rough jute stuff,
Resists the blue, so more gesso? More linseed?
I will make something of this canvas yet.

Now! That curve suggests a woman's back—
More to the left—stripe the spine! Yes, Yes!
The queen is well protected on both flanks.
She scatters pawns like stars in the sky!

BURNING THE TRASH

Down along the damp, light
Freckled path to the spot
Where the fire is
Contained in a basket

Of rusty wire, the
Trash is paper, bagged, carried
Past a six
Foot bank of ivy, green
The green that green
Can grow,

And calls down the sky
The honey-suckle
String pulled slowly,
Brings to a
Point
A drop
Of milk thin honey,

So the trash burns
Ash on air,
To float on the breeze
And settle
Past the edge
Of the rows of young corn.

TRAVELERS

This blue and heavy buttoned coat of Navy wool
Is speckled with paint that won't come off.
I have worn it, a companion, where I go,
People thinking me poor in the falling evening light.
The street-lamp seems to click off when I pass by.
The East River glitters red under a neon sign.
And I am less into division today or trying
To make more of myself than I know myself to be.
I smoke late into the night, dream awake
Of friends and women I know, or knew, or will never know.
But life lived live lacks a sheen, a pearl patina,
And like a diver I can only go so long
Before I need to dive again into the beautiful wreck.
Yes, it is me, and it always has been me if
Anyone has bothered to flag this trail of bubbles.
This is my right leg that is now tingling, so
I stretch out, listen, listening to the hovering
Way people dream into each other in darkened rooms.
And there is the never mentioned spirit-father, who
Got some unlovely bullets in his back. Ticket punched. In
Isolation I acknowledge you, you who engendered this poor
Literal bastard floating and drifting God knows where.

BURNS' WOES

It's some talisman, more of a rusty tanker.
There was plenty, as I told Davie,
Of field to clear, and he got on me
About having both of them in the way.

"Providence doesn't press these shirts,"
I let into him. I told him once and good.
"The moon was the same barren sickle
Both meetings, and somehow we were joined."

"If your father was alive to see this day,"
Davie said and pitched south into the wind.
"If your father was alive," and I half-wanted
To give him a taste of it then and there.

The tanker streamed by, trailed by balloons—
Two balloons, red, scarlet as Clara's cheeks
When I told what there was no getting around.
If my father, if, true—more mouths to starve.

DREAMING ALONG THE PROMENADE
(11TH FLOOR)

You swallowed the whistle the doppel world kacked up—
A provenance, bric-a-brac, generous appraisals.
What was very blank all went into boxes,
And inner storms spilled over the gates into your hot chocolate affect.
Magic marks ran in the basement's sporadic floods.
News: Jesus on daytime; the true archer you once were
Drew blood spores. Powdery blue, an oasis butterfly's

Light clinched wings bespeak twin bubbles you're all hot on.
"If I do this just right," Jimbo said to the Admiral.
There's a French stench of gas and jet in this signifying crime.
The English Suites through headphones: chill out a spell. Verily,
You are you in both these places as we are in ours.
Only the orgies get tiresome, and long. Wretched when
You play at praying, your body spent like a spike

And your knees skinned nasty bad. You're neither home nor away—
Though together your own two lips touch: Miracles can boggle.
And the coven of headless mannequins score
Shop-front windows where grace has fled anon.
Sadly, we all differ only in proximity and posture. The butterfly
Alights. Everyone hits the ground. You're on your own,
Now. Thank you. Given the option, the billboards say, fly.

TRAILS (JULY 4, 2003)

Quill across blotter goes, salt and honey sandals.
Directive: CLOSED on the chain-linked lovers' lane.
Co-ordinants coded: David Arrow Pattern
Flamed along our arms—strike at a distance.
Safety of round-eyed lovers out of sight. As a girl
A poster told her "Loose Lips Sink Ships."

I was third to make my mark, just south
Of the borders of dreaming my love homeward bound.
There was not supposed to be anyone left around
At the given co-ordinates, radio prohibited—
Even the lion's long-secret frequencies a no-go.
SNAFU here—you're on your own, Bubba.

But when Josh went down crossing the clearing,
I dragged him back to safety, brother to brother.
He coughed his last from his lungs.
The rest is a haze through the smoke of years,
But that look I saw darken his eyes
Not all the rye in the world will drink away.

IT HAS BEEN SO LONG NOW

Those were but songs that ran through my head.
You swept the cabin at dusk and hung
The baskets blossom-side-out. The kudzu
And a few insurgent jonquils took the place as we spoke

About lost cities and why the legends
Defined a strictly textbook world but never this one.
In the end, there was wax paper, burnt moths, and several
Revelations pressed beneath the tangled vines—

And we went along with it
As if we were indulging it.
To see how far it would go.
But the vines did their magic, in episodes, engulfing us.

We could have—ahem—escaped.
It's fun though to drink the water we have from the canteen
And crawl out where the last dripping leaves rise up
Like faces in a scary carnival.

PLAN FOR THE DAY

Let that thought flutter off
And not take root in your chest.
It's best just to check in with someone
To lift your voice out of the gravel,
And not become a stranger
Who would range in ever-widening circles
Like a bird of prey, if not hoodwinked,
Hearing unfamiliar voices
Of people passing beneath its perch.

If only the museum of your life
Had a floor-plan you could follow,
You could spend the whole day drifting
From trauma rooms to the long sought
Destinies lost among the pastel villages.
But for now—and now is forever—
Assign the empty crossword blocks of time
Tentative answers, like a stretch of portraits
You will neither remember nor forget.

A PARIS SENDING-OFF

You swallowed the key: Information embedded
In your hair, eyes, voice, and just walked off the set.
I called out your ever-changing name,
Swaggering with my flight glands all lit up
And my hair growing down into my eyes.
You—in the dark—tried to sweep the voices
Like embers back into the fireplace.

And one voice,

"Love can make mannequins move, distances
Close, closets open, windows widen, eggs do
Riotous acts of ever giving forth the freely single
Ever-living gift, a brood, each following
Each into the deepest, palest horizon, parting
Like your own lips, tongue wetting, crushing
Mouth to mouth, till the shell is finally broken."

Fifty quid for the woman in the window.

YOU WHO NEVER WERE

Back, way back when,
I longed to visit you at dusk
When the rain was talking softly,
And your wicker basket
Overflowed with plastic apples.

Then we "Wished each other well"
And fell into the loops—
The lemon grins of pick-up joints,
The no getting past go on the trains.
Society bars random connections.

Outside, at least, the fall
Was losing its petals, blossoms,
And sycamore leaves. Small dogs
Cruised through the black wet night.
My shoes went squish squish squish.

I saw you in the dead
Mannequins in Midtown, dressed
In the sheer colors you liked
When summer had come and gone
Like a stranger, handing you a gun.

DESTINATION

The city swallowed me whole like a long, squiggly bait,
Though I tell less than the truth very often.
My professors complain of this, my syntax.
My artist friends say different things depending.
Lately, I dream of silk: black silk
Tied around my eyes, and being led somewhere:
To a hellova party where I am always just arriving,
And, being blinded, I stumble and fall
Like a long ash into some stranger's drink,
Like counting back from a hundred under chloroform,
Like ether dripping on my scalp, whispering goodnight.

FULL FATHOM

Under the green lotus sea and smitten to boot—
A love you swallow like juice and methadone. I see you better
When these wet letters and our rear hatch escape
Ladders are our only hope out.

I write when I can, but the depth charges
Make my toe grind in my boot. I doubt they realize
We are only young men with mass-produced women
In our steel lockers to help morale.

Under the sea everything is blind. We have valves
And pressure chambers, but only The Man
Gets to see anything of the surface,
But don't get the idea we're crying in our issue pillows.

And so it goes; and if we do manage to get together
We'll carry ourselves around as quietly as we can.
But for now, it's ration tins and Lovely Rita.
A dream, tied off, hitting blood first try, my nodding, Love.

SUNDAY AT THE PAVILION

I have low blood pressure, so
Sometimes my hands shake when I smoke.
Still, nicotine makes things go still when it hits.
I go from smoking to ping pong room,
Till the nurse finds me and guides me
Like an overgrown child to my own room: #417.

Leather punch… squeeze steady and shazaam:
A nifty belt to show the folks at home,
And to keep a souvenir of madness' novelties.
Arguments about what station we'll have playing,
About who will get the extra pudding
Just sitting there on the tray ready to explode.

Morning takes my temperature and wraps
A velcro cuff around my bicep. "Did we have
A bowel movement yesterday, Mr. X?"
"Yes, ma'am, we had a very firm bowel movement."
And here I am again seasick and sleepy, shuffling
Off to someplace I think I must already be.

LETTING IT HAPPEN

Near sleep beneath the glass rafters of the half-way house,
You would come to me as I had asked:
Woman of my other half, which side do you prefer?
You sidle up inside into my left or right
And work your healing magic in the darkness come alive.

Night nurse, angel, whoever you are you, visit me
In the faces of strangers. Now, I've come to see you
In passing, and once or twice I've even known
You in the cunning of your changing incarnations.
I let myself go crazy, just to sleep under your glass rafters.

THESE LIVES

I hate to split hairs, but
I have you to keep me from turning
This thing my way, its business end I mean.
And when your hair's all tangled,
I speak the words that calm your fingers.
Destiny is mostly eggshell and ash.

On your crutches,
And while you were doing your hair
I confessed I'd felt for all
You'd been through and sauntered over:
Half-grasping one shoulder blade
As if you were a wounded bird.

We swallowed the feathery sunset
And spit the morning's toothpaste in the sink—
Swirling down the stainless steel drain of blood.
And these things in my hand are never told
Like getting busted for cherry bombs—
All the small explosions I cherish, one by one.

CHARTED GROUND

I have been watched, charted out as you say.
Marriage would be long in the prospect.
That's fine. The fire in my mind conjures still
The girl who jumped eight floors
But turned out okay. Later, I would eat
Cutlets with her and her parents. She would
Remain in a wheelchair the rest of her life.
The talk was animated and later
I would roll her out to gaze at the moon.

JERUSALEM

Whatever they found,
She'd given me—not the other way around.
I was on the balcony, dreaming
Of an old man yelling
That I'd blown both his speakers.

I hadn't so much as touched his system.
His voice was all in red,
Though that depends on your edition,
And a thousand thousand crosses
Strung along the road.

AMBIGUOUS NUMBERS

It's that in the rain, we could lay quietly
And lean into and against memories of times
When light crowned us, before we counted the ones
In such rich abundance. The locust shells I would gladly
Peel from the sycamores of your really bad days.

And all the water that washes back the pills
Goes brackish blue through the grassy Florida inlets,
Burning off the fog of terminal boredom
When hope is a scarred manatee dodging miraculously
The motorboats of last green good-byes.

I'm sorry if you didn't like my songs,
My asking again and again the metal questions
Which make one all too mortal like the tin
Ghosts that circle around the glass bowl of shelter,
And in a sweeping storm, are afraid to knock.

FIRE INSURANCE (ALL SPRUCED UP)

To be afraid the way they light the sky—
These they call the enemy, is like a situation
Of being alone in the cottage and swatting
Flies that symbolize our higher mystical rings.
The metal hooks onto a crescent
Moon-faced multiple lieutenant who is always checking
Us over to see that the words of the book
Are carried out despite the weather.

Lost in the gale, the wind thrashed.
My Love and I talk out an understanding, see.
If only one of us is to live
I can wear drag like I'd like to anyway.
My Love shall tie herself to a tree.

That's how it goes in the city, when life
Really dishes it out, and you want to look back,
But can't, owing to worn mythologies—
Pillars of salt: the hollow reed bit.
Still, I hook the bloodworm on the metal barb,
Casting past the surf break,
As far away as the great silent one who
Showed me how to set the hook so it sticks.

MUSIC THERAPY

Frankly, when you crack me open
Not much changes; I catch your backspin,
But it was a while back and I didn't let on.
I being a client fresh from Pine View.

You visited, of course. Still, I was interested
In the fashion designer who jumped eight floors
To land wearing a pearl necklace
She got tangled in the spokes of her wheelchair
On the ward of the nineteenth floor,
And the suggestive way she'd jangle them,
Without colloquy, stirring what sex I had left.

MY LOCK

My lock is the joke of the neighborhood.
They come and go as they please.
Yesterday I was missing a pizza.
The day before my cat
Mistook me for someone else.

All the little ways we hurt one another.
Even now two doors down they're laughing,
And I laugh too,
Like someone very tall who has bumped his head
Getting on the bus, knowing he looks stupid,
Trying to laugh it off.
My lock is the joke of the neighborhood.

THE FAUN'S EARS

Is he a damaged or a damaging person?
Sometimes people have to paint things out
To really turn inside the twin lock and key
When fog clouds the higher mountain roads.

I don't get it either this time,
When the weather goes even the way we
Want it to and the tableaus, the moods
Could somehow be heightened by our presence.

But what is this good and evil thing? And do
Cross-purposes yield some other third
Which may be petty theft. My woman
Will get you that way, drawn as she is.

Drilling a hole in the locker room of Life
To see into lives tethered to their respective poles—
We too mill around the center circle,
But never crushing anyone, ever beneath us.

POETIC INVESTIGATIONS

Looking at this

        I pray

               The emptiness won't find me

               Wanting more

WHERE WE LEFT OFF

There was something on your breath, reminded
Me of my youth taking too much X and wishing you'd
Move so my hand wouldn't get sore. I remember
Pods and fluff in a sunken garden where my
Smell thing and my taste thing got really botched. I can
Still make you out with that mouth always forgetting
The wisdom a certain Lama I knew in a previous incarnation
Before I pulled the Thoreau thing and swept the floor.

Blah. Blah. Blah. And of Hesiod. The classroom with
Your light brown hair sitting beside your friend. I smoked
In the hall and could just imagine that stuff, taste it even,
Because my smell thing and my taste thing got really botched.
Attached lobes, yellow hello, hairs beckon
Above your line that the waxing mixed, wiping up the spunk
While the red silk on the bulb caught fire and you cooked eggs.
So what if someone or something is just not right.
I can't sleep with them always building this damn grid. Chicken sandwich
And your glass of milk. These knuckleheads have botched
The whole affair. Go on sleeping and mumbling to yourself
And they will spell it out for you.

SEBASTIAN

Occasionally light will coalesce
Down from your shoulders
And gather into a flag of honey
And pearls, and the villagers
Wave to you going by until
You step out into the long, wet grass.

The archers stood up all at once,
Drew the arrows of childhood
Dreaming into the space below
Your breastbone, and you knew
It was already decided, misguided
By directives as they were to
Connect the random dots.

Idiots they were, marked you,
And went about their business.

BORDERS

She has to fill up this book because
Her teacher said so. She prefers unlined paper,
Like so many of us, because the violence,
Loosely organized, allows her personalities
To spill over into the margin. And in secret
She thinks it's all crap, a concoction of caca concocted
To jettison the box of eagles and crown the crows.
She wants something that, like, speaks to the derelict
In her heart, but doesn't, like, necessarily jimmy the door
And insist on seeing her that minute.

I see her point. I wish people were more sympathetic
With her. I mean a snicker's a snicker. And how would you
Feel if you woke up seeing everyone's favorite number
On their forehead, knew without prior knowledge that
They had a sheepdog named Madison, and Madison
Needed a trim?

And I'm always leaving notes in her box. Things like—

"May you
Drive straight and strong the bitter nails.
Raise the wall.
Protecting yourself isn't a crime, it's a responsibility.

Love you,

X"

Little notes like that.

NOBODY TOO

The things you want to have,
I can't give you.
And the things in you I love,
Are the things you try to hide.

And you could say this back to me,
And nothing would be lost.
And nothing would be found.

When people ask
I can't tell them what color hair you have,
Or what color eyes.

I'm not saying I don't think of you
In the way people call love,

I just have a poor memory,
And I get lost in these dreams.
Happily I know your voice

Calling as I half-close my eyes
Staring at the spinning ceiling fan,
Talking to each other, the way we do.

TODAY

Today I asked if you were there.
Your roommate said you were in the shower.
She said she'd get you to call me back.
I waited but you didn't call.

I cleaned the bathroom sink
And got something in my eye that burned.
I picked up all my empty cigarette packs
And threw them away.

The blinds I put up Thursday are still up.
I'm glad because I spilled the screws
Opening the packet and could only
Find two, so that's all holding them.

I kept hoping you'd call,
But I got hungry and called Tom, your ex,
We went to the brick oven pizza
On Court and 1st place and ate.

WATERTOWN ARSENAL

I successfully suppressed a cough
Through the longish second act,
Fixed on the dancers in their final bit.
"This is Not an Exit" was painted on the doors.
The thin wrist of my companion was hogging
The armrest—the pit, the patter, the slow
Diminuendo of someone shutting down.
"All this was once all in somebody's head,"
My companion said
Then flushed a powdery coral red.

SONG OF THE INK, FEATHERS, AND FOWL

I remember the days in long, woolen coats,
Chuckling against the board where they marked
Oriental progress in yellow straws. The cadet had
Leveled them out even, and so we drew. You saw
The badges glint in points through
The glasses we passed between us . Another mink stole
Was wound off a young bride who skittled here and there
Knocking down high-scoring pens for our team.

You told yourself you belonged. So did I.
We had the prerequisite lab-work done, and afterward shared
A half-carafe, enjoying the omen of a brown-eyed fly
That somehow swam down the glass throat a moment—
Then up and out—doing no one any harm.

For the people in the gallery, though, the frames themselves
Were maybe better than the portraits. The road was closed.
If you'd told me once, you'd told me a thousand times.
The road is closed.
So I found some non-permanent purple rinse
To make myself up for purposes of ritual identification.
I voted for the candidate my role supposed I would.

Later, after he'd been kicked out of office, and his
Wax efficacy was propped up to melt in front of the window, some fellow,
Very officious came by and stamped my thesis in triplicate.
And so I'm trying to get in touch with a friend far away, reliable
And dark as a skein of silk dropped from a tall building
Amidst all this commotion and mixed company. The way
The rain tags it and makes it fall faster
Is only, my love, a matter of resistance.

THE MACHINE

When the duplicate of my love
Confuses herself over the machine,
She slips income into a slot
And comes out pressed into so
Many versions of herself that she
Cannot find the original her—
After several hours sorting through
Various proofs to find which one
She is, she leaves it to me to judge—
To me who has already been
Through the machine and no
Longer can distinguish myself
From my many imposters.

AN OATH

On oath I paid for this by getting
Shucked sideways through the mix
Paid the engineer to punch
A stoned thought in behind the glass
Paid for the new thought
In evisceration of sensual pleasure,
Friends connections sex oblivion,
Paying for the signs
Happened so fast
A river, a cleft formed
Lizards and girls and slit-eyed goats bobbing by,
Dreams of contracts, offers and acceptances,
Clauses promises lovers patterns
Vertigo and 7 tones to adopt in saying
5 things that will bomb being too in my own head,
Beauty of old refrigerators
Beauty of technique a two-finger clasp forgotten
Eviscerated
The long kiss, the dilated eyes
Granting entry narrowed down
To pinpricks, sharpened nibs, quill tips
Scratching over documents
Left hand blotting the losses of a boy
Who found "NO" at the top of the ladder.
The separate signs I understood
All became one sign, nothing was left outside
For the signs to even refer to,
Even the sign itself became part of the sign.
I longed for longing, for the dirty word of love
In spite of the whitewashing ritual on Maze Mountain,
Longed for Hazel dowsing over her long forgotten hair
Calling up the cool, dark waters
Japanese calligraphy
On the inner arm of a brown-haired

Woman in a store
Selling plants
Where I must have been today because
I apparently have some sort of plant on the table,
And there wasn't one here this morning.
Yes, and it was afterwards I caught that flash
Of Hello
In whoever you were,
Wherever we must be meant to be.

THE DONKEY'S DREAM

O, what is the grass?
Blades strewn through space,
Rooted in the shards of glass
Of a portrait's face.

O, where then is the ground?
We left it long ago,
Totemistic mound
Where pagans show—

O, what do they show?
Twin rivers gone to sleep
In an infinite flow,
So the crops they reap

Grow tall and into us—
People born of doubt,
Who don't get all the fuss
Of what it is about.

O, then, what is this "it"?
Things that are believed,
Things that are writ,
How conscience is conceived.

THE LARGE GLASS

You trace designs that move ahead of you
And color-code language rose and blue.

With instinct, reptile-like, you count down.
A fool you ever were, but those in brown

Wreck your green legend to turn your map—
Your David tracing of future hap-

penstance—into a joke, a blank white card.
You know, and knew, the world is cold and hard

To strangers, travelers who can't help but see
Things not as they are, but things as they'll be.

O, sing the song, sing the song after.
O, sing the song, sing the song after.
O, despite the insults and the laughter—
O, sing the song, sing the song after.

BOOK OF LAWS

Dream it into the pocket of the jeans.
It's clear you are beyond my ways and means,

But when they close in I still feel compelled
To steady the picture, keep the frame stilled.

A swizzle-stick (my love is hardly a sword)—
You never vainly take the name of the Lord.

And the last cadet is now off the plane.
Not *everyone* is headed to Maine.

I stick here because of my money thing
And code words of an *Elevator Sting,*

Routing the circuit toward the brown source—
You've always preferred Ouija to Morse,

But your sliding hands take it as a game,
And I am not one to take that name.

PART OF THE HITCH

The last wig of smoke floats across the room.
If you haven't been yet, you may be soon.

Dark scarves of yesterday lined in a drawer,
Knotted in a dream, and no one's sure

If yellow will go with you this season.
No one's sure of your whereabouts or reason.

The scene was wired white: a camera flashed,
And the pockets of feeling that you stashed

Off in the quieter portions of the sky
Were divvied up without a reason why.

Now you only count in groups of three's—
Lost in the falls and endless trilogies.

TURN THE KEY AND SEE

Turn the key and see
What you saw before.
Gravity pulls the body
Through the trapped door.
But thought races on
Like a majorette's baton,
Spinning its own symmetries
On hands and knees.

Brace yourself against a rail
And the waves still knock about.
Wind buckles the sail
And shore voices shout:
But lost in the howl
Gravity pulls a long scowl,
And thought is free to voyage out
Where no craft can turn about.

And after supper in your chair,
Sitting by the window
The breeze tussles your hair
When it blows,
But thought floats over the lawn
With no body to rely upon
And alights on a magnolia tree
Rid of any gravity.

GUITAR

This guitar is where I plug in
To spend the dimes of pain,
To make a little rain
And today I'm well dug in,

Letting fingers list where they will,
Find a moment's station,
Find a strange elation—
Hush the wild nerves, make things still.

It can't be done by will alone—
Crush the crush, make it smooth,
Find the sweet spot in the groove,
Find the marrow of the bone.

Sometimes they come out, sometimes not.
Sometimes the walk leads home.
Sometimes you walk alone,
Knowing you paid for what you got.

O CITY

Movement, here, where it's intended, now—
O city, we have left at last.
You never thought we'd do it, allow
Us to tear ourselves away so fast.

You didn't have time to block the way—
Change schedules, search our duffel,
Arrest us and whisk us away.
O city, we've had enough of your trouble.

Here there's gray mist dusting the hills.
Here the well is deep and black.
We've had enough Chelsea thrills
And friends who don't know how to act.

The trees know who they are.
There's no self-doubt in the ground.
And no one is flagging down a car
Drowned out in the dying Village sound.

REVELATION

Dark is the watch's sweeping hand
That portioned out these days,
Which obey no one's commands
In a house where no one stays.

Spangled through the window's square,
They are ruin half-asleep
That comes down now from everywhere
To steal and reap.

They are the blind man staring
Too long into the sun.
They are a drunkard's swearing
With a loaded gun

Fired into an abandoned life
Too empty to be hit,
Where strife yields to just more strife
Biting at the bit,

Shy white horse of a long afternoon,
Shy white horse black out the sky soon.

"WHERE IS YOUR MOSES NOW?"

You left me in my seat
With two pockets of change.
This Scotch tastes of peat.
My girl's gone strange.

Bandana of my love
Covering bright eyes—
The moon strung out above,
Everything, love, dies.

Visionary flies tell
Me where you've been—
Tied off in a bathroom hell,
Up to tricks again.

EVEN AS I SPEAK

A year ago I saw my other half—
Not wife, a stranger, pass in the street.
I see her a lot, but never laugh—
Or give a sign I'd like to meet.

Have you ever tried on someone else's face?
Feel the angles of your cheekbones change?
What are you? A freak? There is no chase—
Just random dates and dots to rearrange.

But still, now and then, I see through eyes
I know aren't mine and walk away,
And you would hardly recognize.
And now I'm scared she's here to stay.

WHERE THE DUCKS GO

As if the grass is always breezy,
And every oyster coughs up a pearl,
And Life's edict is just take it easy
And meet yourself the right girl.

But the new counter is speckled black,
And the toilet doesn't want to flush,
And a local patriot has built a rack
That the neighbors say is hush-hush.

And in the green room the actors laugh
And switch into drag and kiss and wink.
One's leotards spotted brown giraffe,
One nears boiling on the brink.

They drained the pond in Central Park,
On the rock you can still climb to see
Unleashed, two large dogs of fierce bark.
Seems by their scent they're onto me.

LAST MEETINGS

Where have they all gone?
Away, my friends, away—
Not even one will stay.
Not one is staying on.

I'll go through each name.
Not one will still be home,
And wherever they roam
It's really all the same—

Not so much as good-bye.
No good last supper out,
No telling their route,
No telling where or why.
No way to notify.

THE STING

She took away my urge to say
The language that the happy speak,
And I was silent most the week,
A few words muttered day by day—

Mostly for cigarettes or spare change.
A new one on the block I was,
Asking things of strangers just because
Everything had turned out strange.

She turned my senses inside out,
And I never knew her name.
It was an elaborate game—
I still don't know my whereabouts.

But I'm haunted by a face,
That fails to fade with time,
And though I never committed a crime,
I no longer have a place.

I beg, count dimes, trace my path
Back to find my other life,
And in the midst of all this strife
Whose is it, I wonder, whose wrath?

THE SONG WARD

The last are swept away
And get the chance to sing
To the same song every day
When the clear bells ring.

Traffic outside the wall
Never reaches them inside,
And people seldom call
The ones who hide.

They've washed us of our names
And cleansed us of our dreams
And taught us to play games
Where nothing's as it seems.

And call them on their plot,
You will not last here long,
But if you're here or not
You can't escape the song.

EXCHANGE

I have seen guilt,
Swallowed whole the leaves
Before they wilt
And die on my sleeves.

I swallow whole
Radishes of shame
Until each garden hole
Knows me by name.

I've bitten anger in two—
Breath held
Until I go the rose and blue
Dead friends weld.

The small tree, lonely,
Unseen in shade—
The currency only
The lost trade.

SONG ELEVEN

What's it like to be in pain?
Brother, sister, friend,
With no one on whom you can depend
To listen to you explain
That feeling it's forever Sunday night—
Mid-evening, neither today nor tomorrow,
Neither this week nor last, neither left nor right,
Neither hot nor cold sorrow.
And the doctors can't take it away—
Paid to listen
To your blacks and blues and grays
As the blood inside you glistens
And would seek a way out
Down through the drain
Or some more lyrical route.
Eh? So what's it like to be in pain?

FOR A BROTHER

First in goes the cooler and beer,
Next the tackle boxes, the cushion seats—
The best hour, sunlight dying, is near,
Then the oars and poles, then the feat
Of pushing off and not tipping over.
Dreams of the twelve-pounder, citation-
Sized bass caught on a purple worm,
Following the commission's regulations:
Not dynamiting the pond. I squirm
Still at hooking one in the gills.
You'd know it and automatically take it
As the darkness falls over the hills.
You'd ease the hook out bit-by-bit.
We've been fishing this pond long enough
To know how we both behave on the water.
We both know you're tough
When it comes to the necessary slaughter
Of trash fish such as the long-toothed pike
Which cut in on the fry the bass feed on.
You ask for beers from the cooler like
We are partying at a club till dawn,
When the lights die down, the water's still.
Yes, I see that leading out of your line.
"I see it! I see it!" I say shrill.
The fish are striking. The evening's fine.

VOCATION

They have ways of finding out,
So you'd better stick to love.
They plot out the route
From some vantage point above.
And if you value your own life
More than the gifts you bring,
Get entangled, get a wife.
Do anything but sing.

CUT OFF

I like a bar where there's no line to piss,
Where you don't have to wait an age
To get a drink, where they don't diss
You for the week before's dumbass rage
That filled you with some mere political point
You mouthed off in a huff from the cuff
After stepping outside to blow a joint
Knowing for certain that you'd had enough.

JANE MAKING RAIN

"Hello, Outside. I thought a note
Might make it a little wetter.
It's raining and I'm getting better.
Whatever's doing it don't—ahem—gloat."

Jane's like the girl with the cymbals
Stuck in the way way back.
Jane seems like a hackneyed hack
Because she functions largely as a symbol.

The violinists are quite prominent.
The brass section is seen.
The bass is strong and keen.
But Jane's percussion's an elephant

Stomping at random now and then,
But mostly just flipping manic scribbled pages
While the conductor writhes and rages.
Jane hits blood, crashes hard again.

OF COURSE YOU CAN

You are a railroad spike.
You wear a chain in the rain.
You pour a drink to stop the think.
You rest until you take the test.

You file the cake you bake to make.
You suck on ice which isn't nice.
You like to roam and not go home.
You count your blame, it's all the same.

You talk in pen again again.
You wait until they get it straight.
You boil eggs until they begs.
Your tongue is getting hung.

You fig and pear with brown despair.
You count your hands to understand.
You throw confetti at the yeti,
You feed the dog tied to a log.

You keep the secret tight as fright.
You lift the stone all alone.
You head East for a six–course feast.
You have done your deed upon a steed.

You stop and go like a bruised toe.
You can't find one you could have done.
You face the tricks you can't fix.
You take a wife forever life.

You can't go on with this song.
You stop hard with a quick retard.
You are nice to count the rice.
You must defend and that's the end.

SUMMER IS GOING

Summer is going by heedless of my wishes.
June is a creamy moon.
In the sink are a week's unwashed dishes
Which I always will do soon.

Women pass in less and less.
Summer steeps them brown—
Mostly jeans or shorts, sometimes a dress
When they're headed out of town.

I run between two therapists,
Not knowing what they think,
Then head to the bar to squeeze a lime twist
On the rim of a drink.

VANTAGE

This steeple I feel is falling,
And feeling is a word.
I've spent my turn stalling
Another of the herd.

Someone has set a net
To catch all these bad dreams,
But it didn't get this one yet—
Slipped through the seams.

CITY BLOCKS YOU

City blocks you. Time's not turning.
Streets you watch stop their ticking.
Something somewhere is burning,
Fog comes down to give a licking.
Could be the island's firing—
This kiln's not hot as your desiring.

Fun house animals released by owners.
Rent the house in the fall.
You ask a friend for a five-spot loaner
To watch your team play ball.
City blocks you; white horse is high—
At last sails in a final sky.

BUILDING OUTWARDS

"So it's like a Russian Doll?"
The professor jeered me.
"No. That's not it at all."
He didn't fear me.

"Actually it expands—
Not some figures closing in."
He took my hands
With a grin.

"Though not in the way
Of entropy, but different shapes
Of polygons fitted to stay
Eternally." Arguments to escape.

I pressed on: "Picasso started
At the center and worked out,
So our abstract space is parted
With what we humans are about."

He offered to buy me a drink,
But I had left out the key
To guide him to what I did think.
"No. This one's on me."

DUE TIME

The way into it, if you want a way,
Is to unsay everything you meant to say—
Turn it inside out, like your pocketbook,
And as the contents spill have a closer look.

This is the way the river floods its banks,
When the Dog Star rises up through the ranks
Of winter midnights, lesser stars.
You drown out who you are in bars,

Drown out what meditations keep
From coming out, wandering in your sleep
To seek me alone, here in my dream
Set on automatic. Fingers work the loom.

And I don't answer your knock at the door.
Separately, we do our chore—
You with your hair down and darkened eyes,
Hypnotic, like tulips, together we'll rise.

POP

Flat-top and a clown
Johnny's bringing me down,
And I bear this loose, dark cross
To sway and toss.

I know pop from honey,
And I know well the money
Seems cut grass, low and flat,
Like a circus barker's hat.

But you may have caught a glimpse
Despite the neon blimps
Of a message of love coming through
Games played in the blue.

I know what speaks to me
And however many people see
Doesn't make it worth any less—
Another fine mess.

THE DOOR

She's used this secret door
To escape each pain
Moving in silence over the floor
Into the rain

Her body eases her mind
As she passes into spring
With worries left behind
Death must bring.

But now the door's locked
By someone from outside.
The clock tick-tocked
Oblivious to what had so defied.

Boarded her world to keep her in.
Still the door won't give.
Could someone know where she's been
And so chose not to forgive.

CONSCIENCE

If your conscience resembles the weather,
It flickers off in the light, first to the left,
Then to the right, like a lost tail feather
Denying gravity's heft.

The stars turn to protest kept:
Wisdom through suffering, Aeschylus said,
But protests leapt
From the belt that left its marks in red.

And angels can dance on a pin.
And what is kept.
The scribe scratched his back again,
Rolled over and slept.

Now black and white, hot and cold,
Tint on tint an angel darkling,
And one who knows who is so bold
To ignore a star's serious sparkling.

MOVING

Engine moving fast, quickened clay—
Today is still, cogs conked past reckoning.
We are dispatching this report to say
What is allowed is posted on the red door.

Paid for: this energy atop the edge—
This energy atop the cusp of water signs,
Where meaning curls and dies at the ledge.
Someone is swimming too far out.

Take the heat, August streets—
Motions sluggish and dull
Like Sunday winding sheets—
Quills scratching us slowly home again.

If it's hot, swim.
The cotton cries where it lays,
And the gray garden grows dim, stupid even.
And this, our car, is mostly driving itself.

WINTERTIME LOVE

Wintertime through your checkered gown,
Flecking with frost your long, black lashes,
Tending the fire as it burnt down
The season of ashes going to ashes.

And holding each other in the snow,
And deep, wan kisses in the sleet and rain—
It all seems a long time ago:
Minutes, seconds, days, all that remains

Grains falling through a dying glass—
Undoing your skirt's long bone pin,
Which all autumn long had held so fast,
Undoing your cold sheets and climbing in.

Now will that be all I see
I mean more as a question to call
Upon you to answer back to me,
My wintertime love, my friend in the fall.

WALLFLOWER

A carnival it is still, the old affair
Dressed to kill as people stare.
I don't care what they think they know—
I'd go happily, happily I'd go.

I'd trip over backwards in black-lit clubs,
Swaying to a DJ's dubs,
To beckon you out onto the floor
To dance and dance and dance some more.

THE ROUNDABOUT

I have ridden the roundabout,
Reigned in the horse on a pole
And felt myself spin out
From the center of the fold.

And cotton candy on a cone
Shaped like a barker's megaphone—
Pink like the edge of sky
When the sun dies.

In the fun house I stumbled down
The sliding stairs to face a clown,
Face painted white, red bulb nose
And startled, I froze.

And the devil rang the bell,
And the strong man stepped up to try
To ring it past heaven and hell,
But the devil took the prize.

AUDIT FOR THE FIRE DELAYED

Please don't confuse my impishness with evil,
Or my evil with impishness; my falseness
With goodness, my goodness with falseness, lest
You reflect this misunderstanding back at me and I

Talk myself into a hole. What was once clear
To me now confuses us both. Whoa!
What shameful motive I had
Will trouble me sick on the subway home. Know

If we get detained in a wannabe octet, I will turn
Things toward some goofy theme
No one will misunderstand, where the speaker confronts
My fundamental dumbness and cries.

But you are living, warm, slightly sadistic, and across from me
Glowering. It's silly to think you should consent
To my getting out of it so easily
When an animal trapped must chew off its leg.

THE MEETING

Part of you wonders will
She recognize you. The other part wonders
Will anything be left to recognize
If your imagination matriculates into reality.

Meanwhile, the anti-heroic fountains splash
Your jeans with their idiot spray,
And a blind date is late
In the blonde light that skids down the steps.

And the way these teenagers in their green hair smoke
And band into patrols—the inked
Butterflies
That alight on the small of their backs and drink,

While everything turns a naive cream and mauve
That cools and drags the sky down like a song
To the top of the stairs, where, through the columns,
Someone is waving.

THE ROOF OF BELLEVUE

There are picnic tables on top of Bellevue.
An uneaten crumb of bread beside me: even pigeons
And gulls sense the sickness, though likely it's the cage
Keeps them out. Inside is a zoo of pacers,

Starers, vexers, witchers, spitters of hexes playing with gum,
Hunters of half burnt cigarettes, would be roller bladers,
Misunderstood peacemakers, fazed soldiers,
Sudden feelers up of womankind, and the Male Goon Squaders

To keep it all in check. Last week the World Trade Center
Was there. Now it's gone. I used to use it for directions
Coming out of the train. Now I fear I will never find you again.
My feet haven't touched the earth in over two months.

Love, this is written in the bleached sunlight. Forgive the skimming
Shade of my knuckles as they inch across the words.
I am nowhere else than here.
These stories, I fear, may leak down from these heights.

NOT SO FUNNY

Not so funny, two tall buildings halted
To follow us down when the pails swung wan
In the gazelle game, "By all means of protection—
Regardless of how.   Kill to effect ratios intact."

Unto the lies of the Giver, be you
"Pleased enough if she survived the dowsing
Of the pancakes and the collapsing Inferno,
Instead of being caught in the act."

Both of us get hungry and change conditions,
As with the weather so with us. They cannot be sure
Enough to say we caused the given "weather"
To be how it was, as with the suspect's *mens rea*—

Our shared condition, to cool the judge like a codpiece,
No exit but to shake it off, to carry that weight—
Lucky to accept this power of acceptance,
To accept the brute fact all of my friends took turns.

STUMBLE OF AN OPERATIVE

You attack the verb "to stumble" like a lobster claw—
Same way I do, and learn to crack it open,
Like someone practiced in a given given,
Splattering a canvas with lemon and butter.

People try too hard, as a rule,
"Apply Themselves"—to stay in the quick of things.
By design the vectors are hurled and deflected,
Are channeled to innocent correlates of bystanders' nape nerves.

Else our nicks and knocks would be noticed—
Assigned proximate notch-to-notch, point-to-point embedded,
Flags of Red Dinner Napkins, specific warnings
Here in the brute circuitry of Paradise.

And the shit's so involved: our best people are still
Scaling the towers of the bizarre boot camp into the house
To reconstruct positions I reassigned, but the country meals
Of usurpers stick to the ribs. Eh, my dove?

THAT GROUP'S FEET

That group's state of mind pulls
People and cameramen up through a secret function—
Soul pathway, into the Big Blue Marble Pattern.
Wow! Mom! Ada to Eve! Shoveling thorns

Into twisted shapes. New Virus
To declare against. Agencies keep hush hush—
Establish the parameters of what love we're building.
Le Roi de L'animation, Blind Tiger Pattern.

So our man is holding down 11 floors. Angelic Combat,
Someone lithe sliding down the chute. I can live without
Privacy, but the routine whisking at each bar of dragonflies, &
The buzz of black wings, mock, mock, and mock, gets me.

And when there's some available, we're not interested,
And usually wait till 3 a.m. to talk down some lazy-eyed woman
Back to my studio: Spanish guitar, Sor #5 in Bm,
And the sex I don't want but take like ice in sweet sweet tea.

IN THE HALLS

In the halls you tried to match the swinging hands—
Navy hands, attached to cadets full of codes.
From you was taken blood and maybe little songs,
Snags looped under the eyelid, to wrestle down a dragon.

Later, you ranged through pool halls, marking tattoos—
David Pattern Arrow (distance and musical stones),
Marks confirmed, over years, our youthful canines flattened
Until the biting down turned to a spitting out of darts.

And now, Dear Bandana? To know how the rungs
Of the wrongdoers were hemlock spiked, not by man's flat logic
But by ruthless angelic fire. What I took, Love,
I paid for dearly, by not partaking of the festival.

I hope I helped you dodge the letter killeth thing.
I can't tell us apart at times—Adam Cadmon #3 routine,
But I trust you are somewhere with a date-of-birth,
As I walk the dragons that hide, most of me, away.

INTERLUDE IN SHOWER TILE GREEN

Is more of a means towards an acute destination—
The process of getting there, getting recognized and processed
Into the # 0, or by multiplicity the #1—
The I.D. scraped loose, I.D. x 0 = John Doe Rigmarole.

Love is what can't be said, the Tao sputters.
My eyes nervously glance away from your hoodwink.
In the bathroom where the ants make off with hairs—
Your icy blue—nobody's home—cool as a milkmaid eyes.

Rita—God, it's doggone frivolous up here
Above the flattened canines, with lions and bears,
The thick lore of the dragon: loses its holy whatever.
They've seen me shoot. No one will play me in the movies anymore.

I've been under this major Houdini spell of late.
Under the dying citrus circus tent, where CO_2 seeps down
From the towering lakes killing early noonish risers.
In our plaid skirts, I would essay, my love and I escape.

SOMEWHERE, SOMEHOW

Somewhere, somehow the band played on—
My Darling—in the shared movies of our minds.
You went dashing from sentry post to field,
Finding welded fast a metal arc, bent to pray.

Really, you halted to mumble
And fog the air with silent tongues. The prayer
Of action lost momentum at the scroll of a crest—
Like some heady thing loosed to the wind.

This is a valued pox: applied correctly
Would make more of us both – whoever
We happen to be now, as we learn use of this fire—
Like the taste of going down on you the first time.

Things sublime like that, Gazelle. I guard the tower
And wander like a dazed cadet from taking the hits.
And life can be wonderful, all buttercups and cows,
And this lion's claw clefts the devil's chin.

SWALLOWTAIL, YOUR SLIGHTEST TOUCH

I like to mark 'em up myself. I scrapped
In the loft with the younger ones to get here.

That new high-test line, it's all I use. In season
(If a body hide a body), I squat in the blind.

I reckon ya'll be comin' this-a-way.
I reckon a bulge could be a silver flask.

But it's just nerves that quilt the spots
You can't reach. Histamine inhibitors

Provide symptomatic relief. There are no bugs
But the ones the Littlest Princess in London exults in.

In her cotter-pinned box,
She keeps exotics and accidentals no one can see.

Beside it are the tweezers, needle, pinning board—
The ether she's always knocking herself out with.

THE GOOD MECHANIC

They drained the old mill pond,
And the pickerel dug into the mud. The time and place you
Were born into, the obligations to God and Country.
You swallowed the message and found
Death wasn't like dozing off on a train; it was like
Stepping up to a podium and just going blank.
God is mostly small things you don't care about: the fleck
At the bottom of the sink, a red ball, the black
Eye of a chickadee.

I know you have a fundamental objection to this,
But I also know
You would gladly return to a time when everything was a new,
Sleek animal that licked your face. Lifted by
These swells, you tap a glass, cup
Your hands around a piece of coal. You think if you
Press real hard, you'll make a blackbird.
Maybe so, but as it is written,
Let not this book depart from thy mouth.

THE PARIAH

I would point my finger at fate,
But to face facts I can't escape from taking
The blame on myself. At the table I find the dish
Bitter, which others seem to find so sweet.

And I would gladly exchange this solitude
For a touch, a few easy words, only to belong
More to the people I strike as odd, as having
Nothing to contribute to the conversation.

But my patterns make me walk across the street
To avoid meeting whoever's coming, to avoid making
Eye contact with strangers walking their dogs,
Or young people gathered around a stoop.

And the policeman there seems to see through me,
Is vaguely aware that I am somehow out of step
In the dance of life, and as I turn the corner
His footsteps in the silence grow louder behind me.

ANOTHER EXTREME

I have decided to be, but can't
Escape from the fact I sometimes need
To be around others, just as sometimes
I need to be alone.

I get depressed when I don't see friends,
When no one calls for too long.
I start thinking it's because I'm nervous
And talk too much when I'm excited.

I forget that place
Somewhere in my heart where I slip off to,
And which is half my problem,
Because I need to focus on the external world,

Which makes for more engaging conversation,
From what I gather,
Than these swans and this stillness and whatever lake
That I, for one, am floating on.

TONIGHT IS JUNE

Tonight is June thinking it is final.
The last of the instruments has turned to gold.
The gold has gone into a chest
Lowered through the sand without value or color.

June was over the waters, but the glare of June is gone
Which had moved among so many symbolic fish.
But June's fish to June were nothing but flashes
With silver backs that winked atop the puzzled waves.

The eyes of the fish could never look away
Long enough to make a wish the way June had done
The moment she became a white bird and rose
From the dark waters to which she had surrendered.

On the shore, in the drizzle, an empty hammock
Still wags between the trees like something
Indentured to the weather that is always blowing through
Everything that is not asleep and everything that is.

SOME OTHER LIVES

It takes a little orange to catch
The sickle shape that slowly
Becomes visible under the eye
And shows who's in which tribe.

Their shapes give them away.
You draw them, when they come,
Into wondering what it is
You are doing in this corner.

They see you're scribbling,
Or drawing a picture—which makes you pale,
Suddenly, as if you've been
Swimming and being underwater

Has followed you into the air.
And what's really there will always be there,
Though outside of the picture, outside
Of even the frame.

SO WINTER ENDS

So winter ends and the scorched earth
Various agents helped make our life into,
With our help, becomes more subjunctive.
The facts dance, were to be

Dancing, having met an impersonal force
Allied in squadron formation. The meaning
Found and lost all becomes one, disappears
Like a train into the sun.

Hello the chronicle, the kin charts, the cant,
The hollow keening for the hapless and hunted,
A pattern of something to be taken away,
Dittoed and reduced, again. Hello logos!

You can talk about what you need to,
Practice your forensics thing,
Like you came to life from a book,
And just can't figure how to get back.

QUIET ONE

You were always about to say, but
Never did. You lived life off to one side—
Like someone trying to even out the weight
Aboard a boat none of us knew we were on.

Too much drilled into you.
That other wisdom lost—two can make a team,
A flannel shirt can mean a better year,
A frigate will roost.
Quiet one, 2 a.m., thinking of you.

SO VAST, SO BEAUTIFUL A LAND

A grace note, a slow country feel. But it had
An agenda, a red glare thing going on. You could see
Trench-lines, and think of a woman
Who existed on a grainy, flat, historical scale,
Without key, or hope of structural revision. Because
It was how she felt at the time, she moved
His spirit, rippled the wheat as the storm approached.

Later, after it was confirmed, it was conducted by postcards.
They met and talked of amber waves, alabaster—
Things like that. That was before he apprenticed himself out,
Learned faux-finishes and brilliant sheens.
Years passed before she ran into him, and they
Talked about the exchange rate, what it would have been like
Had they ever given in.

This ended the lesson,
And I wanted my way out of the Great North Woods,
Out of everything that was beyond me. I wanted
A fast train to a city where my life was neither sung nor torn
From the pages of a book. I had packed the night before.
I awoke in the light, clutching the soles of my feet,
Contemplating a discreet universe that allowed
For strange connections, green hair, Helen Keller.
But later, at the platform, the train rocketed by
As if it had something better to do
Than stop for me, a ticketed passenger.

SHOULD I CALL HER THIS SOON

Reading "Whoroscope" on Sunday
1 p.m. in blue boxers and a Jerusalem T-shirt,
Having gotten up to smoke
And brew in my dirty

Coffee machine, the glass pot of which
Is lurid, I reckon that must be the "light"
Coming in where the cat
Knocked the blinds

Askance in the night. In arm's reach,
An empty bag of caramel-covered popcorn.
I ate its contents (packed by weight) yesterday
Five-ish to rally my sugar, and got

A piece lodged in my ear.
"Christ," I said, "Anthony'll be by
In five minutes to go to the BBQ,
Yet I have caramel corn stuck in my ear."

FULL-LENGTH MIRROR

Somewhere there's a law
One can't wear a mellow shirt
And talk about one's feelings
On a summer night with a friend

Or somebody will keep
Bumping into one to order drinks
When one just wants to eat corn dogs
And drink ice water and cool off.

In the backroom an oily
But ruthless construction floats
On the water of Pauline prescriptions.
One wants to eat soup

In a size XXL cartoon T-shirt,
Singing in a kilt that shifts
Below the bagpipes one plays crossing
Hudson for gazpacho.

RIVER'S FLOWING

River's flowing high this year—
Flowing strong and dark,
Round the bend to nevermore
And passing by the Kirk.

The flashing teeth of river pike
Spread open like a girl
Are as bright as polished steel
And twice as surgical.

It's not the river's fault
He harbors subtle snakes,
Or sometimes swallows Jimmies,
Michaels, Johns, and Jakes.

River's flowing high this year—
Flowing dark and strong,
Round the bend to nevermore
And turning into song.

RANDOM BEES

Random bees are crawling over a gray card.
You lifted honey there, far from the hive and felt
Lost ever after, not knowing yourself
From the silence which formed on your tongue.

Innocence strummed a zither to the lost tune of faith—
Summer movies, ultramarine—all called you out,
Last and lost. Blinking in daylight,
You filled yourself in as the music rolled along.

I know now what those times meant,
Tall and drunk in the rocks, where no one ever
Denied you went. I know now the river
Is fast and clear and on its way home.

Run now. Run back the way you came,
Where the rice still falls with a quiet intensity—
Back where we belong, or tell ourselves we do,
Like gulls at rest on less predictable evenings.

RESTRAINT AND SECLUSION

All right, you say I think about you too much—
I guess I could think of life outside and clutch
At life, at ghosts, at terror on the cherry-colored rails,
A sailor's promise in the shadow of his rhinestone sails.

I've tried to couch it so you can swallow back
My rather fucked-up life come back from the Sound
And when the running blues strike at metal in the bay.
The more things you learn, the less there is to say.

Always you seem far away, elsewhere, a pretty goner—
The way the nurses say, look on in dismay
As they give you another shot to chill you out, bring
Your silver back to quotidian to alluvium wilt

Silt and mother's milk, O Loner, My Gone, My Goner,
The idiot Doctors with their batteries of tests:
Their use of throwing knives—on the boards blindfolded,
The Doctor throws the knives, ink blots. Charts, the team.

And I'm addressing nobody else but you, you know
Who you are. You're scarred and scared, and this exposure.
And you say "I'm nobody but me, and people are
In my world told apart by proximity, but they've tagged

Me with this white plastic band for ID, patient number
Significant to me, I gnaw the thing off first thing.
A young person, you moved much too fast, chronically
Wearing boxing trunks, sitting in the sparring rings

Where you fought no one but the shadows, and dodged
Each blow you threw at yourself, almost.
Your doppel hearby evinces it has survived: oranges
Like women fair-haired my wounded love went down.

And when one idiot sees another of himself,
Who is to know which one is the real subnormal McCoy?
And how did this structure get built? No one knew
It would get smacked and go full tilt. You may like

How these silly lies belong to the future, drawn
Here and there on the sidewalk and through other mediums,
Just to keep us—for our own good—from going
Through the doors where visions step up, for real,

To shake hands. I won't drip through the faucet your mamma.
If it wasn't you it was your doing all the same.
And I really like the way you dress and drum and stuff.
I was, granted, upset when you came in with your plated seasonal

Of blondness wet from the shower, tresses disheveled,
In the same relic dress of red and blue unraveled,
Each hair numbered, by whomever for whatever purpose,
Each brow even, the smallest, thinnest Picasso dream.

And lands on the back of your hand like a given mark,
But one you blow away the tiny thing and make a wish.
And I wait to know your name, especially now, with summer
Coming apart at the seams into the dream we may both have

Of having a roof over our heads, that's with the usual "T"
Left to bear the brunt of July's transgression. When we
Talk like this, I can't tell which of us is doing the talking.
Part of the joy is in part the frustration.

And part of the failure is part enervation,
And it's good to pocket the umbrellas from red iced drinks
For conservation and fortune's sake. I know from scouting
Missions there a swallow where you are, at least during   ➜

The seasons when the campus lawn isn't touched by frost.
And if we mention a desire to escape, it all flows and follows
They think we're serious souls, like them, with their yapping
Dogs. Even the great bear, Ursa Major, must stay clear of

The dragon's path as we find ourselves again inside
The old factory where the underground mimes, mirrors of
The mine, contort themselves unto ridiculous renditions
Of who and how far they manage to think we could get.

And I see before I wake this collapsing layer cake I think,
As a civilian would, of you tossing your bouquet
Over your shoulder into the agape mouth of the rain,
And the pain paid for in this bizarre currency in which

The safety glasses square things off, square the circle
Making everything gray and OK again.
I wish I could get a note through to you, to make it
Worth all the recycled energy—the flattened canines

Of our jeering and keening kind, which likened us to
The lyrics of a fifties flat top car long due for inspection.

PRE-RECORDED MESSAGES

It was through neglect
You wandered off and found yourself
Picking up a frequency seldom used.
If it were all in your head, it would be
One thing, something other than a nonplussed
Acknowledgment of what you spelled out
With your decoder ring, small box of shards,
And the family crest someone shattered
In a frosty ball.

Don't throw your hand, just beware of wild cards
Held by silent, nameless players. Just because
The mountain is quiet doesn't make it less than a mountain.
Though the young ones tend to bluff, they are
Rarely called.

Know the jack of hearts and the suicide king have
A pact, and the forecast can't be altered just because
You don't have an umbrella. Try
To treasure simple, honest things, and keep
A straight face with airline security. Witness
Protection programs exist. But you won't let on,
Even though it makes you laugh, like you
Have a parachute or something.

PROVE IT THEN

Sure the board is rough and splinters
Sting doubly in the tongue, but don't deny
You need friends and sunsets bordering
On obscenity. Clouds cannot move
Unless the wind…unless the wind

Oh why bother to talk I'm losing it
And the mice leave tracks and make me want to say
"Globe," "hollyhock," "sea shuck,"
But it would be looked down upon
The way a bouncer
Looks down on the blind man, smelling musk
Between the blades of a table

And when the tree has shed its silk,
And the potato winks its little black eyes,
Then and only then
Will it come together, will the reason you left
The blanket of leaves in the trunk
Be apparent. It's the way you choose,
Don't complain if the only people
Who touch you are swingers

Ho, Ho, you there, in the mirror
Crowned in your horny diadem
This was written so you would know
I am utterly insane
And have received your latest transmission

If this had been an actual emergency….

"Richard, it has come to my attention
A set of triple-beam scales is missing
From the lab. Please see me at once."

And I wish I too was good looking,
That cork sank, that the big man didn't
Make me do this to you.

                    Tentatively yours,
                    Adam Kadmon

180

MOVING TO MAUVE ROOM (DEVICE 32)

I simply need latitude. All these
Devils you sense I brushed from my hair.
And love, I like the sparks you strike
On the asphalt every afternoon when I swallow
Everything the sycamore offers up and things

Skimmed things off the top. I have
Deleted the connections. Leave it to a bright girl like you
On a night filled with interruptions to make them.
Don't trust me, put up a purple sign. You don't
Have to give your number out. Use discretion.

Inheriting a fortune does this to you. Little Larker,
Mother's sure you're born for the stage. I'm a humble
Electrician, but I like lights, tinsel, spectacle.
I'm very good at complex mathematics and suffer spells.
Two gray doves will come to you in three weeks, be

On the look out.   Please don't
Be put off by hesitation—I am naturally shy.
I commune with the dead, have interests in developing
Countries, enjoy the company of young people, and
Talk to myself. *I love you all, I love every one of you.*

PROFESSIONAL SCHOOL

When honest
Dark birds get bleached I dream
Of circles red and green, of marks
I meant to hit to triple the score,
Of sections below the welded grid,
Of horsehair chairs, of bristle, of whiskey
Of nights she'd shift things
Around with her shirt open,
(Of Illyria being beautiful, and in the checkered rain)
Shift and slide a horsehair chair
Away from the radiator
To keep the horse's checkered mane
From galloping into the checkered rain.

My new friend says forget her,
My new friend is growing annoyed.
Forget her
The way
Gradually the patients do
When the tags around their wrists
Are cut and they go blinking through the doors
To put the yolk back into the egg.

(Before they had tugged in private at the band,
They wanted nothing but to be outside, to start again,
But the band was their mark, they dare not escape.
The band would get them sent back.
It was the band that held them back,
But you should see them, on the curb
Even before they've been shuttled home,
They feel their wrists, rub nervously for the band.
They need to be reminded who they are.
This person is only your wristband.)

I do not know what my new friend wants of me.
I don't know how my new friend thinks of me.

My new friend says I need
That I need someone…who…I forget what…but mainly
To be corporate and sane with, sublet dog run something affirmation stuff.
My new friend says someone who calls
Collect from payphones on Tchopatoulas Street
Is not someone a professional needs in his life.

But I answer anyway, to the rings, when she needs
Sensitivity and pleads me to remember
How life brimmed over once
And was taken to the square to see the promised riot. And meeting
We'd shake out a taste from a paper, withdrawing
Some place where I was suddenly in
The mirror with her, palm of hand to back of hand
In white noise pipes drown it out,
Faces effaced.

("I did something once,
For this jerk for a picture once.
He said the rushes weren't
What he thought they'd be.
He made promises.
Speed freak loser.")

I think of her.
Her one yellow eye that stayed half-open while she was sleeping.
I think of her yellow eye
I think of her yellow eye a lot.
It was extremely beautiful high.
The pupil was not quite centered.
She showed me.
I wouldn't have noticed it if she hadn't shown me.
It is what I remember best about her,
About life in general.
I am depressed,
And each day my tuition gets more and more expensive.

BOY

One thing I fear is not so much
The usual awful feelings. It is the plain silliness
That sometimes comes over me
When I am feeling nice and comfortable.

I have been burned badly
Often when being giddy,
And am most open to being harmed
When I am madly laughing.

I will always make this bed neatly, tuck
The four corners in tight before I crawl
Under it, where I hide
Some pieces of a light I broke, where nobody

Will look. But if they make me explain,
What will I say? *All the king's horses
And all the king's men?* When the days in store
Would teach me the lesson without their help?

PASSAGE

These tokens we hold onto
We were told would take us through.
So say something now, something so the dream
Will go better, something so I'll know you're there.

The long hair that grows in old pictures
Is growing still wherever it chooses,
While in a smoky van someone is laughing,
Leaving fingerprints on each thing he touches.

And the way stuff disappears gets to me—
The way old peoples' belongings are boxed up,
The way the things I have touched and loved
Will also be boxed up, sooner or later.

I walk through things never having seen—
Smell without smelling, taste without tasting.
And the old woman is outside my window
Begging for quarters, who will leave nothing behind.

ONE MARTINI

You expected some beatnik
Giving up the spirit
In a mediocre, though celebrated,
Stretch of dust and rails.

You can shave your head, startle
People with your piercings,
But this is too, too something.

So you move on, hoping the free buffet
Will be replenished, and the waiter will drop
Whatever he's holding

You know
It's bad when they spoil your fun with a siren.
You've got to play the part, walk the line,
Talk like everyone else.

FIRM CONVICTIONS

If you really want to, go ahead,
Piss in a cup. But there are still unlisted
Opportunities, and true travelers are worth their weight
In glossy editions, not to mention the panoramic view
And crash 'n burn legacy the deal affords.

Far away is fine, but the landscape is always the same—
Red and hypnogogic, before you drift off. Water
Is purer near its source, and visions go hand in hand
With oxygen deprivation. Stars zigzag like gnats,
An identity dissolved in a Tunnel of Light.
You tend to get caught up in it—want to give it a name.
But wherever you go, the horizon moves at precisely
The same pace. That's the point really, isn't it?

TROPHIES OF THE SUN

I'm writing you again, though I don't
Know if this will make it through
The firewall or get pulled the way the last one was.
One never knows what the machine will flag, so

They are always calling me in. As per our last
Communication, I'm still being watched, but
Even when they know I know
They are friendly enough in passing.

"After all," someone said, "We're all on the same side
Here, Chris," (what they call me). Since you asked,
My job description requires me to rotate
Often and aimlessly and to pretend I'm legally blind.

They can't keep people where you are?
Try the turnover here!   It's a slaughterhouse! Your
Survival depends on not being able to see the butcher,
And not being willing to hear the crows.

NOTES TOWARD A BETTER LIFE

The sheet of a score and a saucer of milk
For a cat and a composer—shackles and shells
He codes by tensile strength and hue. Words come through
Cold fogged goggles, from unseen friends away.
This is the ritual of the composer's fallen house.
This is where the rain falls against the floor,
And where, at last, he sees a clustered fist
Of frost lights in the distance. He places trust in them,
Crumples up yesterday, and tosses it in the river. It floats
Over the mindless falls, turning into some minor
Variety of madness and mist, entirely out of his hands.

THE MAZE BEHIND THE PALACE

Providence, provincial town, studying junk bonds,
Which was called our education, the past burning
And wearing a gown, brought us somehow together.
Duke of Gloucester Street, hollows midnight peopled

All dancing toward a reckless revelation—
Tallow burning in the windows of the Inn
Where the type of people slept who were against us.
That fall, while they were in the stadium, we coupled.

Safe and Warm had been fine a while, but with you
We ate X and harvested something strange
In the Sunken Garden 4 a.m. Afterwards, you lingered
When the hall's early risers might have leaned

Hard into us with their hazing, but hushed and sleepy
You fled to a class on derivative markets. O for that lost,
Oblivious and tender Saturday, helping you fold laundry—
Tobacco flecks on your lip, the dying rain-colored flowers.

MONSTER DE LA NOW

Little epiphany, satori, punch drunk—
Mais oui, he goes too far out, losing the listenership,
The DJ is pleading his way,
To be more into the production of parachutes

For his audience being well, keepsakes of totally there—
(Note to point, fact has us compiling from North 19)
The sins of men in a Paradise of Assassins—Hash Marks.
Darius and Delueze. Hi. I'm in the tomorrow business.

And so hell with imputations and color charts—
I've got the coordinates up here, Captain, typography my forte,
The maps of days when you'll pass a given given
In the east and long a little bit to linger dangerously.

So the hooves are talking again, as we ode into the ship—
Special forces who freeze up when being seen.
They come unglued at the slightest…but when the time comes
They pierce the visor slant, emerald banners shining.

"But until I can protect myself better,
They will continue to steal my parts. The smile
Thing went quickly, rendering me, as they say, 'flat'
In the notes they make remarking on the lack

Of affect upon my countenance. The heart-screws,
Too, were among the first things they took, though
Gold, they were just tiny things the thieves melted
Down—the bastards—more for pleasure than profit,

Leaving my heart exposed, to do its heaving business
In public. Two punks rolled me for my feet,
But I found the one with the fallen arch in a dumpster
Nearby and reattached it in a makeshift way,

Far from satisfactory, which caused me to hobble
Off to find mother. This did, however, distract attention from my bad
Teeth, which sit on top of my stomach because some teenagers
Made off with my windpipe, one night, laughing
And swinging it around like a segment of hose."

MILADY'S (10:00 P.M.)

The lightest possible touch was your first one—
A stray tassel of braid of a hair spindle,
A string boat sculling leeway,
Saying "Hey" over the smoke and water fog.

The bar was full of the sweaters of October
Cuz the drab weather broke today—
And umbrellas were huddled in a corner.
The foreigners were looking at their shoes

Like the people whom we eye
In the red cashmere and silken brown hair,
And the looks I stir up in my anomie
Toward you in the latent bravado of the scene.

Old checkered cabs and their cornering power—
The waitress came out with buffalo wings,
And I sipped on a long–necked domestic beer
Nor entirely for you, but close enough, Love.

MAUVE MUD PIE

That week or two of mauve mud pie
Seemed worth the cost of nearly dying.
Now the pants I wore are scorched—
Stained with blood and beer and semen:

The humours of the market's season.
Actually, there's some mustardy-looking stuff too,
And a streak of something like sweet and sour sauce,
And an exploded pen mark at the zipper.

And a wallet with no I.D.
(Which I opted to fling around 59th Street)
And at Federal Plaza: Driver's license, two school I.D.s,
two dead cards, #'s for two deranged women,

Gym and karate cards, all went into the pool,
All went into the fountain of Rockefeller Center,
As I distributed my identity and purchasing power,
All for the taste of mauve mud pie, nearly dying.

LOVE KEEPS GOING

Love keeps going, point is,
Around terrible corners, chucking hubcaps,
Leaving me to doubt
Its return.

Not simply its returning,
But the fact of my lover's pale leg
Half out of the dark
Limo window.

By her thigh she's facing
Toward the river, her chin extended, cocked
Like an old Colt aimed
Into a stranger's black blazer.

I put coins in the slot,
So the show will keep going,
So she will come 'round again,
So I might have a turn in the black blazer.

KARLHEINZ ON THE COVER

It's hard not to wish I could spike
A point now and then that wouldn't matter
The same way I wish your arsenal could dowse
These residuals like sparks into a pail.

It's almost easy dreaming into this—
Playing Joseph Cornell to some of the garbage,
The alchemy agenda, and in assigning proper value
To the manners various programs "seek to foster."

It's that this world, this base, is like
A bag of beans which will take
Too long to soak and so stays in the back
Of the cabinet for the next occupant.

I'm usually picked last
Because I have trouble wanting to keep the ball
In play and serve it too often
Into the phony, predictable roof-beams and rafters.

I TURN AWAY

She turns away each time the same
To see you with a silver crest or wings.
You doubt you'll ever know her name—
Ever see, say, taste, or sing.

She is the mockingbird above your cot
Where you lay down till you're through.
Conservatory in a public spot.
You remind yourself often, you do.

But they are people worn by the weather.
They are not frigate birds or deer.
They whir off in a flush of feathers
Caught up by fear.

Angel Orange stalks the green river
Where you will arrive one afternoon's ride.
If you should find a feather left by the Giver,
Pick it up. Look. She is on the other side.

THE FLIGHT

I met a man, a pilot.
Said he'd take me off the ground.
He made the offer half in jest
When no one was around.

The moment we went up
Until we leveled out,
A bucking quest for strength or faith
Or what it was about.

I felt something in me give,
Climbing through the air,
The things that had looked large down here
Appeared so small up there.

The whole flight seemed a spell—
An injury, a grudge.
But whether or not I'd had enough
The pilot had to judge.

GROWING THIN AS PROCESS

Shut up and kiss me
Is what it can take
To wreck an esthetic in mid-July
Before it drives into the desert to grow

Bearded and shower and admire itself
Nervously in the restroom,
Sulking
And eating trucker speed.

Wide-eyed it feels for scars
Thinking
Someone took a kidney while it slept.
"And faith, save the nothings I taped

In the window to be lost. They
Have been bitter, little crab apples
Like the type we chucked at everyone
Who ever climbed toward you."

GREEN WILDING

Like a table in love with the floor,
Even with everything under water the way it was,
Sharing a space and knowing each other's
Mother tongue and root locks, provided stability.

I've crossed out a lot. For instance, that star stuff—
Days in brown, escapist modes, and #2 pencils tipped
With standardized fire. Such lost fugues
Flashed and hushed, exist now

For part of us is still there. Lost pictures can still possess,
Can still lay a patch to your soul pan
And back to the world at large. They can dreamscape
The most literal lagoon. *I gave you sugar for sugar.*

And there's pavement here, despite the sycamores.
Lots of magic can heal the year's favorite bird.
Tracer fire and nitrous. The long term assignment is
Nature's way back home through you again.

FANCY CLOTHES AND THESE ARE ROSES

From early on she was picked on by maelstroms,
In her teens she was affected physically by Rimbaud,
Someone once told me, which knocked me out,
Thirteen years ago in a stranger's kitchen.

A dreaming junk in projected winds of Authur,
(Do it yourself I'm sick and somewhere else)
Almesbury stage adrift, pale and gifted throat,
Floating over the boards like Rilke's dying swan.

You seek the echo's source in a wardrobe
Where hang a bandage and trowel from Jung's castle—
Hope you find solace from what troubles you. It's worth
A botched life and pain to help folks, regardless.

A student writes: "I saw her once, with my
Boyfriend Todd. The guy in Gambit said
The show sucked. Todd and I totally disagreed.
We thought she was like really different."

RESIGNATION

She was lovely, more blackberry than thorn,
And between the V of blue paisley
A map of freckles unfolded as she leaned close
And put my digits into her machine.

Balefully, knowing she wouldn't write,
I spaced out on something shiny
And picked up a California roll and watched
The jazz singer and swirled my ice around

In a hardwired broody-moody
Brought on by a storm of strapless things.
Thus rudderless and reverent with deep lordy gaga,
I bubbled quietly through my straw

And was changed to a Dolphin called Bumpo
In a big aquarium, where she was watching me,
Saying to her friend, "Look! Its eyes are so human.
It's like…it's trying to…tell us something."

DIALOGUE INVOLVING GARMENTS AND ACCESSORIES

"Why, Jenkins, that shirt! It's remarkably sane."
"Thanks. My wife picked it out."
"And that tie! It just exudes sanity."
"This? Just bought it on sale. Silk."

"I've never seen a saner pair of suspenders."
"A Christmas gift from my daughter."
"The overcoat, too—sensible and simply sane."
"You've seen me wear it before."

"That watch is ticking along very sanely."
"It's nothing fancy."
"Your underwear, no doubt, both comfortable and sane."
"I hadn't given the matter much—"

"Frankly, those shoes are a stroke of pure sanity."
"It's kind of you to say."
"But Jenkins, it's clear to me that you've gone mad,
Utterly, absolutely, irreversibly mad."

DEVIL'S TOWER

There are some left in those knotted caves
Who know, it is said, channels back
To your people's world. Jupiter is pulling
Things along nicely, but Saturn's

Squaring it makes the passage problematic—
Like some of the connections in *Zettel*
Or finding a peach pit in your house salad.
Neither terminal unless you

Crack the casing through haplessness or design.
And the brunt of it may lie in ourselves, but a few
Are born with something like a laser's prick
Of barking stars inside of who they are,

Which makes their conversation like fire
One day and Virginia's wool the next: white dwarf
To red giant during the course of a single meal,
Eaten alone, going off at the mouth.

DELUSIONS FROM A BUS WINDOW

So it was just me, longing the way I did to be a flower,
And people were moving to other seats because I guess
They could tell *something* was up, and the stars burned
Like the lights in a university town and I rubbed them to see if

They would come off. And in the back seat, the one beside
The john where we could conceivably make out, a girl listened to
Rock n' Roll though headphones. If you remember me, please
Call my box number and we'll meet at a juice bar in Chelsea.

Finer things broke down around me (my fever was 104 degrees
And they debated icing me). Brother, I had maybe eighty dollars,
Some generic people around me, a photograph, and some time to kill.
I can pull off anything on short notice 'cept I was feverish like.

Emergency room, nurse pokin' around for my friggin vein.
A failed life and a shitty little four-track. I wanted to pop
A dragon. You: shining son, namegiver, emblem. Me: watery rose,
Down by the riverside, down by the riverside, down by the...

TESTIMONY FOR SOMEONE SILVER

Sunday at evening and the light falls
Between yesterday's pages. She has her home here—
In an atmosphere of pink and silver junkets,
Garish Chinese lanterns and horses out of line.

Pale, like letters in a private alphabet,
Orange and purple fish swim on the watery tiles,
Spitting out little poison balls of dough, their patterns
Checked by the grout grid, marked for a lark.

Where she hides smoke is blown through keyholes;
Injury is seven drops of tea
And there's a litany of other crimes that keeps her busy
Sweeping a path through, to where all this will stop.

Here at the dark end of the hall, the rain is falling.
People in colored slickers talk with their feet.
Outside, outside—where she spends too much time.
Even now, in this quiet room, the fireworks far away.

THE CATENARY

On the island which is connected
To a bridge, you work things out like wavelengths.
You chum and pot orchids, but realize,
Ultimately, there is still the reality of the bridge.

Perhaps you could blow it up. But how to "be"—
Really "be"—with the untidy migration
Of plover and spoonbill and human sorts
Who could potentially claim to be somewhere?

And what about the problem of the bridge?
Better to crack a coconut than puzzle
The night away on that one. Better
To dream and chum and dream some more

Of the maps to countries that don't exist,
Of the continents being somehow wrong, rearranged
As if by an angry child, of something bright
Moving at night over the water toward the island.

OF CUPS AND BALLS, COINS AND CARDS

Outside the house, lost in the design,
I left something at your door—a long stemmed spray
Of something wild. Some blind and minor stars—
Sweet on you—had contrived a sort of pageant.

I signed on as player. The something wild
Was only pretending to exist in this world. Its scent
Became a parade we held hands at the borders of,
A dandelion we blew till it was out.

There was a dragon, a mask, and an airplane.
The fact everyone else was wearing a parachute
Should have clued us in, but it was all so seductive—
The green room, the glitter, and the pure oxygen.

But that life, thankfully, is gone, fled. Our roles
Rolled over in the ground. Now we walk
The promenade, looking for the man who sells pistachio ice—
The souvenir blackbirds gathered at his feet.

COME DOWN IN TIME

That was the place I hid, in the first car,
Manhattan-bound F, scanning the feet,
And seeking a spot to look where nobody was
As we all went underwater

Between York and E. Broadway in the tunnel
I fear may yet give way in some catastrophe,
And I thought of Howard, because I felt better
Thinking of him and the bowl of hummus

And the lentil soup we had the night before,
Tipping the waitress $9 on a $30 tab,
And Howard saying *Tender is the Night*
Still moved him after forty years.

What moved me? I wondered and closed
My eyes feigning sleep as we rolled into the station,
Where the pair of shoes I had been staring at
Left without saying goodbye.

HASSLING KOOKS

And into this relentless cast of white jackets
Fazed the blurred coordinates with copper chops—
Roger, board taken.   Enemy bishop left to taunt
As crosses stalk the road for show and snake oil.

The sun won, the son's stunning contract,
Woven into a bleeding souvenir, Roman numerals, Love,
Vex your hemline through green bubbles.
We gloss the fact we share our laser in private.

We were secretly upgraded out of mad solo romping
Into each other. The others drowned in a burlap sack, tied off.
We shalt together, whoever we are, taste the sugar cane
In a vague historical fire, a year spent under thatch,

Before it will be as we are currently depicted,
We'll glow like blown glass, get completely hammered
On the anvil of wanton boys, have the secret charmed out,
One for the other, as it was writ.

BETWEEN THE CLOCK AND THE BED

And you just skipped off, happy as you please,
Thinking you'd find a Steinway in the woods. I can't
Blame you, seeing it from my angle. I know the paint
Was flaking on the stoop, the canopy frayed. I wasn't the man
You needed and I'm sorry.

I oiled the porch swing the moment
I was told. The sadness was delicious. But you bounding
With your strong limbs
Should know the search party couldn't leap the stream.
Dumping the silverware down the well was one thing, but
Burning the old bridge so many good folks traveled
To get some small recognition at their readings,
That was out of line. Do you think people
Want to be blindfolded and led to even the loveliest vista?
It makes them feel more like a hostage than the
Guest of honor.

That night when you made your debut
And reeled through the receiving line, was there nothing
Genuine in the warm modulations you took on? Your checkered
Dress, the color in your cheeks. Your voice in the corner
Where you singled me out was all dotted-eighths and quarter-rests,
As if the din of all the people you had loved
Was just a rhythm section existing so we could trade fourths.
So I could grow enamored of your complex and syncopation.

Somewhere down the line, they may decide
To let you into the house. That itself should be controversial
For the myth will not be easily turned. You will be judged like
A British team chipping at a pediment. They will not take the
Weather and advancing troops into account. For
Now, though, it's the knowledge you could have shaken it off,
Could have let it dissolve like sugar sweetening the impression
Of the morning, of the light coming through the blinds.

AS A MIRROR IS BELIEVED

A fine portent of something or other
These long and lazy days lead into—a chink in the wall,
Where you shake the idle hand of a sycamore
That grows outside a brownstone's window.

Then the signal—silence and sigils—
The less than final outcome for someone too long
Outside the circle of light shed by a scolded star, which sulked
Off yelping, tail between its legs, to go dig up the garden.

How else to insure the job gets done? But for now,
The girl across the street is blond. She wears a drab dress
In the rain and dreams in green. She weaves between the white
Umbrellas clustered like phlox at the light.

She is I. I am that young girl. And we are both
Suffering a crisis. And the star and
The dog are, too, though just who is in which room
We only know by tapping at the walls, if then.

TITLES FROM BLACK WIDOW PRESS

TRANSLATION SERIES

Chanson Dada: Selected Poems by Tristan Tzara
Translated & edited by Lee Harwood

Approximate Man & Other Writings, by Tristan Tzara
Translated & edited by Mary Ann Caws

Poems of Andre Breton: A Bilingual Anthology
Translated & edited by Jean-Pierre Cauvin and Mary Ann Caws

Last Love Poems of Paul Eluard
Translated with an introduction by Marilyn Kallet

Capital of Pain, by Paul Eluard
Translated by Mary Ann Caws, Patricia Terry, and Nancy Kline

Love, Poetry (L'amour la poésie), by Paul Eluard
Translated with an introduction by Stuart Kendall

The Sea & Other Poems, by Guillevic
Translated by Patricia Terry with an introduction by Monique Chefdor

Essential Poems & Writings of Robert Desnos: A Bilingual Anthology
Edited by Mary Ann Caws
[forthcoming]

Essential Poems & Writings of Joyce Mansour: A Bilingual Anthology
Translated with an introduction by Serge Gavronsky
[forthcoming]

Eyeseas (Les Ziaux) by Raymond Queneau
Translated with an introduction by Daniela Hurezanu & Stephen Kessler
[forthcoming]

Poems of A. O. Barnabooth by Valery Larbaud
Translated with an introduction by Ron Padgett and Bill Zavatsky
[forthcoming]

Art Poetique by Guillevic
translated by Maureen Smith
[forthcoming]

Essential Poems & Writings of Jules Laforgue
Translated with an introduction by Patricia Terry
[forthcoming]

Furor and Mystery & Other Poems by Rene Char
Translated by Mary Ann Caws and Nancy Kline
[forthcoming]

MODERN POETRY SERIES

An Alchemist with One Eye on Fire
Clayton Eshleman

Archaic Design
Clayton Eshleman
[forthcoming]

Backscatter
John Olson
[forthcoming]

Crusader-Woman by Ruxandra Cesereanu
Translated by Adam Sorkin. Introduction by Andrei Codrescu
[forthcoming]

The Grindstone of Rapport: A Clayton Eshleman Reader
Clayton Eshleman
[forthcoming]

NEW POETS SERIES

Signal from Draco: New and Selected Poems
Mebane Robertson
[forthcoming]

LITERARY THEORY/BIOGRAPHY SERIES

Revolution of the Mind: The Life of Andre Breton
(revised and augmented edition)
by Mark Polizzotti

www.blackwidowpress.com